# The Keepsake Cookbook

12|11

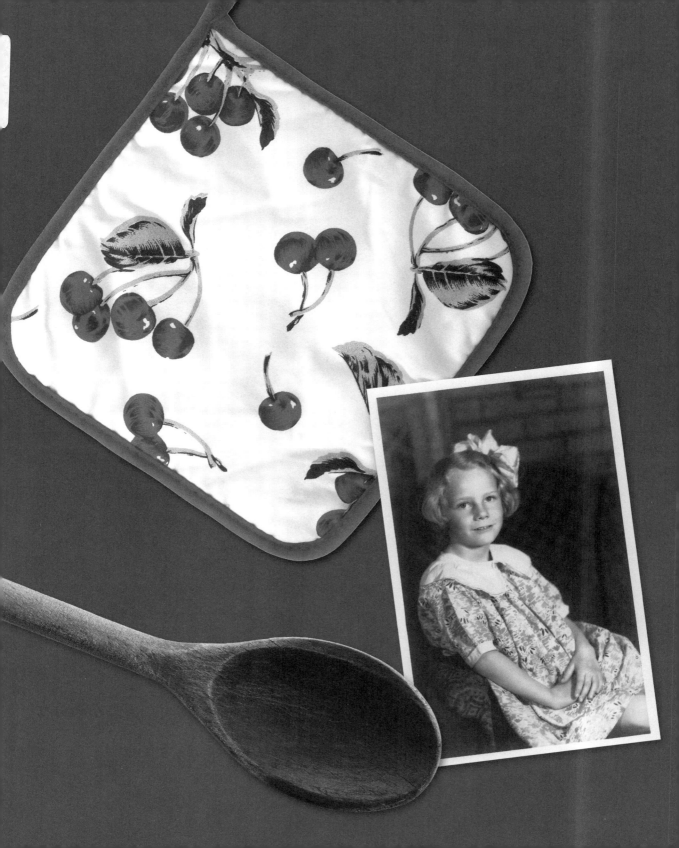

# The Keepsake Cookbook

## Gathering Delicious Memories
## One Recipe at a Time

Belinda Hulin

LYONS PRESS
Guilford, Connecticut

*An imprint of Globe Pequot Press*

*To my husband, Jim Crissman, for all the delicious memories.*

To buy books in quantity for corporate use
or incentives, call **(800) 962-0973**
or e-mail **premiums@GlobePequot.com.**

Lyons Press is an imprint of Globe Pequot Press.

Project editor: David Legere
Text design: Sheryl Kober
Layout artist: Melissa Evarts

Photos from Belinda Hulin unless otherwise noted.

Library of Congress Cataloging-in-Publication data is available on file.

ISBN 978-0-7627-7007-6

Printed in the United States of America

10 9 8 7 6 5 4 3 2 1

# Contents

# Acknowledgments

Many people have shared their kitchen memories with me—some dear friends, some mere acquaintances, some former strangers I met at book-signing events. Their stories touched and engaged me, and this book would not have been written without their inspiration. Likewise, I'd like to thank my extended family for showing me the power that a keepsake cookbook can have: starting conversations, bringing life to memories, and drawing far-flung loved ones back to the table.

My friends Robin Warshaw, Ruth Chambers, and Carol O'Dell offered support, love, and ideas as needed, and I'm grateful. Mica McPheeters shared moral support and her invaluable artistic eye. My husband, Jim Crissman, and my children, Dylan and Sophie, graciously fended for themselves—and me—while I wrote, and some of their kitchen adventures have already become family lore.

Globe Pequot Press acquisitions editor Mary Norris believed in this book and helped nurture it, while project editor David Legere worked his magic, getting *The Keepsake Cookbook* through the editing and production process. Thanks to copy editor Karen Ingebretsen, designer Sheryl Kober, and layout artist Melissa Evarts for turning my humble efforts into a thing of beauty. And last, but certainly not least, a big *merci beaucoup* to agent Bob Diforio for helping this Cajun girl get her ideas out into the world.

# Introduction

Like many people, I always threatened to write my family cookbook. I come from a long line of Cajun and Creole cooks who celebrated life with food, and food with life. As a food writer and cookbook author, writing down my own culinary heritage seemed like a natural thing to do. It also seemed like I'd have plenty of time to get to it, eventually.

Hurricane Katrina changed my attitude. About a month after the storm flooded my mother's house and sent her into exile, I found her recipe collection on a high stair step in her drained-but-sodden home, carelessly shoved out of the way and thereby saved from destruction. Family photos, mostly stored in chests upstairs, also survived the storm. I took these treasures with me, and in the months it took to gut and repair the first floor of the house and make it habitable again, I began writing. For each picture, for each recipe, there were memories of people, times, and places. There were also questions—about relationships, cooking techniques, and recipes unrecorded. As I called on my mother, near and distant relatives, and friends to fill in the gaps, I began to realize what might have been lost. For all the family stories and dishes I'd shared with my children, there were hundreds that simply floated in the back of my memory.

I also began to realize that many, many other families had lost cherished food memories to the storm, and even more families had lost their culinary heritage through simple attrition and procrastination.

As I shared with friends my mission to record my family recipes and memories, I got encouragement. And, I got stories. Stories of a Sicilian grandmother's fig cookies, a Minorcan great-grandmother's chicken *pilau*, a Polish aunt's cabbage noodles, a German-Jewish mother's prune *hamentashen*, and a recipe for delicious watermelon-rind pickles perfected by a thrifty second cousin. Some of the stories came with wistful admissions that the original cook had taken the recipe to the grave, or that there had never been a written recipe, or that the recipe was somewhere at the bottom of a drawer, waiting to be unearthed. Almost to a person, those with whom I spoke about my cookbook wanted advice on how to begin writing their cookbook. Some sheepishly admitted to having purchased "cookbook" software or starting a recipe file, but mostly they confessed that they just didn't know where to begin.

I wrote *The Keepsake Cookbook: Gathering Delicious Memories One Recipe at a Time* to help men and women record their family recipes and memories, and to help non-profit groups and other collectives build their cookbooks. I believe my step-by-step approach will show budding cookbook authors not only where to begin but also how to plan, organize, and complete any of a dozen or more keepsake cookbook projects. In so doing, I believe we'll all be creating heirlooms, but maybe more important, we'll be helping to build a repository of culinary history that's now being lost.

The most important thing I have to share with readers and cooks is this: You can do this. You don't have to be a professional writer or cook, or an accomplished computer maven, to put your family or group recipes and memories in a usable, presentable format. You don't need to have all the recipes or stories together to begin, and you don't have to wait for the "perfect" time to devote to the project. You just need a desire to capture what you do know for posterity.

There are many paths to your cookbook. I wrote *The Keepsake Cookbook: Gathering Delicious Memories One Recipe at a Time* to be your road map. I promise you a delicious journey.

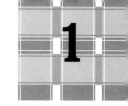

# Your Table, Your History: What Kind of Keepsake Cookbook Do You Want to Create?

Walk past a neighborhood bakery and take a deep breath. The scent is unmistakable. Cinnamon, vanilla, shortening-laced pastry, and the intoxicating blend of ripe fruit and caramelized sugar. It's a simple apple pie, a classic, satisfying dessert. And yet, the aroma evokes so much more than a craving for pie.

An apple pie can call forth memories of Grandma's Thanksgiving dinners, of crisp autumn afternoons in the country, of fireside tête-à-têtes with your best friend, or your own favorite potluck offering. A fragrant pie, or any dish for that matter, can open the window to memories of people, places, and things we've loved.

Food may be one of life's necessities, but what we eat and how and when we eat it are rooted in our heritage and our experiences. That old adage "You are what you eat" actually has a flip side. We eat based on who and what we are. Archaeological evidence and ancient texts have allowed food historians to trace the origins of something as basic as bread to the Neolithic era and to trace the advent of yeast-raised breads to Egypt, 4000 BCE.

But what about the secret ingredient that made your aunt's poppy seed challah such a joy to share? Or the recipe for the homemade cinnamon rolls that came hot from the oven every Christmas Eve of your childhood?

Unfortunately, too much of that essential human history disappears by attrition with every generation. We all know that when Columbus brought tomatoes, peppers, chocolate, potatoes, and peanuts from the Americas, the cuisines of Europe, Africa, and Asia were forever changed. But a hundred years from now, will anyone remember the molasses-and-peanut-butter spread your grandmother made to stretch the family food budget? Or your Aunt Susie's fudge-covered whoopee pies? Or your Swiss expatriate neighbor's crisp-edged tricolor potato *rösti*?

Those are the types of recipes that usually survive, if at all, by word of mouth. Capturing such recipes, including the circumstances surrounding their evolution and enjoyment, ensures that your great-grandchildren and their children can re-create the flavors that make up their heritage. To put it more directly, if you don't teach your California-born children about the maple syrup snow candy of your Vermont childhood, who will? And if you don't write it down, will they remember to share the treat with *their* children?

## Savoring Memories

This book will give you the power to capture your culinary history and your most memorable food experiences. You'll also be able to inspire your friends and associates to do the same. The quest to record old family recipes drives many keepsake cookbook authors to build a legacy. However, the process of writing a memoir cookbook can be applied to many, many different groups, genres, and situations. Your grandchildren will certainly appreciate a collection of your recipes, but so will your friends and neighbors. Or maybe you'd like to document the amazing monthly potluck dinners hosted by families in your multiethnic neighborhood. Or how about collecting recipes and stories from the mouthwatering sweets booth at your church's annual spring festival? You can create a specially themed keepsake cookbook for someone near and dear. You can even make a few dollars for your favorite cause with the right recipe collection. All these options are within your grasp.

**FAST FACTS:** *De Re Coquinaria,* written in Latin in the first century CE, is believed to be the earliest surviving collection of recipes. The book is often credited to legendary gourmand and lover-of-luxury Marcus Gavius Apicius. While the credit may or may not be accurate, the word *Apicius* was later used to refer to recipe collections.

Take a minute to imagine your cookbook. Maybe you want to keep the focus squarely on dishes and dining events. Or maybe your effort can become a showcase for other well-loved activities. A keepsake cookbook can pay homage to your favorite collection, your favorite hobby, your best photos. Some authors will want to practice and show off their food styling and photography skills, while others might prefer to build a scrapbook of life mementos, original illustrations, and family photographs to accompany recipes. Group-authored books can chart the history of an institution or organization, or celebrate group members.

My friends Susan and Rick Cannizzaro are working on a cookbook that merges his original artwork—much of which features coastal creatures and themes—with recipes from her parents' chain of diners, once landmarks along Maryland's eastern shore. Another dear friend, Robin Warshaw, is considering a cookbook to benefit pancreatic cancer research, honoring her late sister. The book would feature comfort foods like soups and oatmeal cookies, and it would have vignettes and photos celebrating the lives of those who battled the disease. And I know that fans have been pestering Florida hot sauce maven Ed Creamer—creator of Ed's Red Hot Sauce—to put together a book of his favorite seafood concoctions.

Whatever theme or approach you choose, there's never been a better time to create a keepsake cookbook. Awareness of gastronomy as an academic pursuit is at an all-time high, as is awareness of culinary heritage and cooking techniques. Born cooks and born connoisseurs are devouring recipe collections. Also, digital tools make gathering and assembling an attractive, professional-looking cookbook within easy reach for authors of all skill levels. In fact, your "book" doesn't have to be a tangible tome at all. You can distribute your collection of recipes and memories in a digital format or post it to a website.

In the coming chapters, we'll talk about how to research and create your keepsake cookbook using both high-tech and low-tech tools. In the meantime, let's examine some of the possible themes for your cookbook. Once you've decided on the parameters of your book, we'll move forward with a step-by-step approach to creating your food-based keepsake.

**Recipes and So Much More**

Think of your cookbook as a recipe collection with flourishes. Your keepsake can be a combination cookbook/scrapbook, cookbook/photo album, cookbook/sketchbook, or a cookbook/journal. Or it can be a fully detailed memoir with essays, vintage photographs, and recipes. The important thing is to tie the recipes to time and place by adding written and visual cues. The materials you collect and the approach you take will depend largely on the type of cookbook you decide to create. Let's look at a few possibilities.

**The Family Cookbook**

Family heritage cookbooks are the jewels of the keepsake cookbook genre, as valuable to future generations as an annotated family Bible or a cross-stitched family tree. These books hold clues that connect modern urban and suburban families to their farm-bound grandparents, their immigrant great-grandparents, and the vagaries of geography and economics that play upon food styles.

Although some authors like to focus on the culinary talents of one relative—say, a Pennsylvania Dutch grandmother who created bountiful meals from meager ingredients, an Italian grandfather who owned a bakery, or a father who perfected his own barbecue ritual—most tend to pull dabs and dollops from the past and present. The easiest way to begin a family cookbook is to start with your immediate family and, as with a family tree, work backward. Assemble the recipes your immediate family loves to eat; attribute them to Mom, Grandma, or your best friend's aunt; and go from there. With that core, you can begin to reach out to relatives for the recipes you remember from childhood and to mine old recipe collections for taste memories.

But recipes are only one part of the mix. The very best keepsake cookbooks include stories that tell the history of the family, the food, or both. Family photos, anecdotes, and favorite sayings make the books fun to read. Even slivers of information—say, an ancestor's name on a ship manifest, a photo of a 1956 Chevy, a baby's footprint, a picture postcard—can all add to the mosaic of an extended family feast.

Family cookbooks can be designed and compiled by one author, or they can become a cooperative venture that grows with contributions from aunts, uncles, cousins, and old family friends. You can build your cookbook one segment at a time or create a series of books by focusing on one era, or one family branch, at a time.

## The Holiday Cookbook

Not ready to assemble Grandma and Great-Grandma's recipes into a weighty tome? No problem. How about surprising the kids—or your mom—with a small but beautiful book of Christmas cookie recipes? You can begin with as few as fifteen to twenty cookie recipes, including traditional family offerings and contributions from distant relatives and friends. Intersperse holiday snapshots from years past and brief Christmas recollections. The year it snowed unexpectedly, the year you got your first two-wheel bike, the year Santa made an appearance in a red suit with Bermuda shorts, the year of the puppy, the first grandchild staring at the tree—these are all wonderful memories to document and share. Do you come from a family of cut-ups? Put together a photo collection of the adult grandkids mugging in antler headbands or your Christmas-sweater-wearing pets. Throw in a handful of cookie-baking tips and you're set.

Of course, you can always go for a full celebratory menu. The family Passover cookbook, complete with recipes for Grandma's heavy matzo balls and Aunt Lucy's light matzo balls, charosets from both the Ashkenazi and Sephardic branches of the family, and special *chametz*-free Passover desserts, would be a great gift to future generations. Add snippets from the Haggadah and vintage photos of family Seders, or pictures of antique Seder plates. Then insert a chart or series of boxes listing the year, the Seder host and menu, and the family member tasked with asking the three questions, and you've got something to treasure.

Religious holidays make a neat framework for church and synagogue cookbooks, religious association cookbooks, and youth organization fund-raisers. Simply expand the idea of family-centered meals and memories into a communal buffet, with contributions from many individuals, as well as institutional history.

For a faith-neutral family or group holiday cookbook, think Thanksgiving. The holiday is a huge, happy food-fest in the United States and exists in various forms in other countries as well. The basic menu of appetizers, salads, side dishes, desserts, and, of course, turkey, gives you a scaffold from which to build a comprehensive collection of recipes interspersed with food photos. Add short contributions from family or group members detailing some of the things for which they're thankful and you've got a beautiful keepsake.

Major and minor holidays abound, making the list of possible holiday cookbook themes limited only by your culture and preference. In New Orleans, Italian Americans celebrate St. Joseph's Day with bountiful food altars to share with friends and strangers. I know families who have created pages chronicling their altars over the years. Photos of the giant food spreads, and the days of preparation, combine with Old World Sicilian and Creole-Italian recipes to make a unique keepsake.

**FAST FACTS:** The first book written by an African American author and published by a commercial US publishing house was a cookbook and household management guide. The book, *The House Servant's Directory: Or, a Monitor for Private Families: Comprising Hints on the Arrangement and Performance of Servants' Work,* was first published in Boston in 1827. The author, Robert Roberts, ran the household of the governor of Massachusetts. The book has been included in the Historic American Cookbook Project collection of the Michigan State University Library.

However, the really great thing about holiday-themed cookbooks is that you can start small—with a Twelve Days of Christmas cookie cookbook or an Eight Nights of Hanukkah latke cookbook—and add new holiday books or chapters as you like.

## The Culture Collective Cookbook

Sometimes groups of individuals or loosely connected families want to celebrate a common culinary heritage, and there's no better way to do so than with a keepsake cookbook. Although the culture collective keepsake shares ground with the family cookbook, the focus is on a shared ethnic and possibly geographic tradition.

For example, Jacksonville, Florida, hosts one of the largest and oldest Middle Eastern communities in the United States, having welcomed turn-of-the-twentieth-century immigrants from Syria, Lebanon, and the Ramallah region of modern-day Israel. The result of this well-settled population group is an American Deep South city where the fresh flatbread, *kibbe*, and kebabs are as plentiful and authentic as the fried catfish and hush puppies. However, as with any migration, the lines between cultures and cuisines become blurred. So my Lebanese American and Syrian American friends who sit and argue about quantities of parsley vs. mint in *tabbouleh* do so in southern accents while slow-cooking black-eyed peas for New Year's dinner. Suffice it to say that their culinary traditions differ not only from their ancestors' Old World recipes but from the tables of other ethnic Middle Eastern communities across the United States as well. A cookbook put together by a civic club or just a group of friends to celebrate that specific community and its signature dishes would be a treasure.

**FAST FACTS:** According to the *Oxford Companion to Food* by Alan Davidson and Tom Jaine, 30 percent of American women collect cookbooks, and at the turn of the twenty-first century, the average US household had fifteen cookbooks.

Likewise, the specific flavors of the Creole Italian community in Louisiana, the Seminole tribe of Florida, the German cattle ranchers of the Texas Hill Country, the Vietnamese French bakers and seafood restaurateurs of the Gulf Coast, the Gullah Geechee descendents of the Carolina coast, and the Basque American cooks of Nevada and Idaho all might inspire those immersed in the traditions to create a cookbook that reflects their unique cooking, entertaining, and celebration customs.

The culture collective cookbook theme works well for an extended family, a civic club, a neighborhood group, or a church with a heavily ethnic congregation.

## The Travelogue Cookbook

If you're like most people, you've got hundreds of vacation photos sitting around in boxes, in albums, and on hard drives. A great way to bring those vacation memories to life is to build a cookbook around your adventures. Your photos and journal notes from Florida will make a great backdrop for the conch fritter, grilled shrimp, and Key lime pie recipes you collected. Your tour of Pennsylvania farm country will yield beautiful photos of rolling fields and recipes for chicken corn soup, shoofly pie, and apple dumplings.

I've known cooks who juxtaposed recipes against memorabilia from all fifty states, adding to an ever-expanding album and making their cookbooks a work in progress for many years. Others only chronicle their trips to offshore locales and their favorite exotic dishes. Still others create albums with photos and recipes from friends they've visited. Carol O'Dell, my friend and author of *White Iris*, a novel featuring Vincent van Gogh, is building a cookbook around the foods she's sampled during her travels to retrace Vincent's life.

Travelogue cookbooks can be an excellent medium for sharing travel experiences with friends—one they'll actually welcome. Vignettes about your experiences, or even brief fact boxes about the locales visited, can flesh out the cookbook. Put together physical books for good friends, or send each year's installment as a digital file with holiday greetings.

For a group travelogue cookbook, try a theme like Summer Vacations or Seasoned Sojourns. Assign participants to contribute either a certain type or certain number of recipes plus notes and visual reminders of their trips. Use scanned maps for added design elements.

## The Collection Showcase

My friend Ruth Chambers's antique doll collection, photographed in different arrangements and settings, would make a beautiful scrapbook. But when I see the dolls, I see a teatime cookbook starring Ruth's signature gingersnaps and brownies, and expanding to include other desserts or light sandwiches and snacks. That pairing of visuals and dishes would offer a true collectible cookbook, and one that could come from no one other than Ruth.

**FAST FACTS:** Best-selling novels and nonfiction tomes come and go, but best-selling cookbooks tend to live on for decades. The *Better Homes & Gardens Cookbook* and *Joy of Cooking*, both published in the 1930s, have sold 32 million and 18 million copies respectively.

To build your own collection showcase cookbook, think of the things that are important to you or those you love. Try pairing seafood recipes with your dad's fishing lure collection or your son's model boats. Your vintage quilt collection would perfectly illustrate a family cookbook featuring comfort foods.

While some collections may not seem to be recipe-friendly (your sixty-three antique brooches?), the fact is, any combination of photogenic items and dishes you love can make a keepsake that will be closely identified with you and your passions. That will make your book special to those who love you and those who share your passions. A gentleman I met at a bookstore confessed that he is building a cookbook of seafood boils and bakes using his tried-and-true recipes and pictures of his miniature lighthouse collection. He already has a list of fellow lighthouse-lovers he met online clamoring for copies.

Collection and special-interest cookbooks are a natural for nonprofit fund-raiser cookbooks. Your sheltie, beagle, or golden retriever rescue group would undoubtedly love to share photos of their success stories and snippets of animal legends and lore, as well as favorite recipes. Sell the books as e-books from the rescue website, or have copies printed to fulfill mail and Internet orders. Equestrian clubs, cat enthusiasts, friends of zoos, museums, and libraries, orchid societies, and bird-watchers all focus on creatures or objects that could beautifully illustrate an easy-to-share recipe collection.

## The Community Cookbook

Homemakers certainly issued their own cookbooks—often under assumed names to protect their privacy—during the eighteenth and nineteenth centuries in the United States, and a century earlier in Europe. However, the cooperative efforts now commonly known as community cookbooks first appeared during the Civil War era. A band of women in Philadelphia published their recipes and cooking tips in an attempt to raise money for field hospitals. The idea quickly caught on, and by the early 1900s there were thousands of cooperative cookbooks issued by women's groups in support of all sorts of causes.

Today community cookbooks are a full-fledged culinary genre. Many compare favorably with the most lavish professionally produced cookbooks. They appear in support of schools, hospitals, women's groups, children's programs, and a smorgasbord of other nonprofit causes. A healthy handful of companies exist primarily to produce these books, handling printing and distribution as well as design and editing.

**FAST FACTS:** The very first Junior League cookbook was published by the Junior League of Augusta (Georgia) in 1940. Titled *Recipes from Southern Kitchens,* it raised money for the group's community projects. Since then, Junior League committees have produced more than 200 cookbooks.

*The Keepsake Cookbook* isn't designed to compete with the well-oiled production efforts of established cookbook producers. However, for some community and association cookbook committees, the techniques here can be of great assistance. Those who are just starting a group cookbook can use *The Keepsake Cookbook* to create a blueprint for their work, deciding in advance what themes, illustrations, trivia, and histories they wish to pursue in addition to recipes. For experienced cookbook committees who want more control over the design and development of their book, *The Keepsake Cookbook* offers plenty of ideas and suggestions.

The very best community cookbooks serve as a reflection of time and place. They capture what people in an area are cooking and eating as well as how they're entertaining and thinking about meals. Although most are broad-based rather than targeted at any specific individuals and interests, they do have a significant place in the chronicling of culinary history.

FAST FACTS: *Larousse Gastronomique*, the well-known culinary encyclopedia, was first published in France in 1938 with noted chef Prosper Montagne as the author. The book, which includes information on cooking terminology, ingredients, and techniques as well as recipes, first appeared in an English translation in 1961. The updated 2009 edition offers 3,800 recipes.

Before planning the logistics and specifics of your group cookbook, do yourself and your collaborators a favor and decide on the core purpose of the book. If you want to commemorate something—say, your congregation's fiftieth anniversary or the retirement of a beloved school principal—your cookbook should focus heavily on elements that give a sense of collective history or personality to the final product. If your effort is mostly a fund-raiser, think carefully about your audience. If the goal is paying for a new roof for the community playhouse, then the order of the day would be stories, recipes, and entertaining tips to appeal to the broad community of theatergoers and theater lovers. If your fund-raising goals are less specific—say, supporting your service sorority's civic projects—then look for a broad theme to showcase a book with well-chosen, well-edited recipes.

One of my favorite fund-raiser keepsake cookbooks was produced by a group of six sisters with multigenerational roots in DeFuniak Springs, Florida. The women wanted to restore a historic house that had once been the showplace of the town square. Spearheaded by one of the sisters, Jo McDonald Manning, the group produced *Seasonal Florida,* a carefully annotated book that has been through multiple printings.

## The Menu Cookbook

Menu cookbooks can be merged with other types of keepsake cookbooks, including gift books, collection showcases, and travelogue books. However, they are especially useful for keepsakes built around the activities of a gourmet club or a group whose members hold meetings at one another's homes. Each participant can be responsible for providing the menu and corresponding recipes for his or her event; then the cookbook editor or committee can select common elements to include in the mix. The elements might be photos from the evening, funny snippets of conversation, cooking tips, or paragraphs on the origins of the dishes served.

The menu keepsake format has one great advantage: It allows participants to build the book gradually, one meal at a time. At the end of a year, everyone in a monthly meeting collective will have access to a twelve-meal cookbook containing at least sixty recipes, plus happy memories.

Even if you aren't part of a dining collective, you might consider building a menu cookbook to share your own ideas about dishes that complement one another, give insights into your philosophy of entertaining, and create a memoir of your parties. I personally have started a menu cookbook that offers themed party fare for holidays and celebrations, including Floribbean-influenced Thanksgiving dinners, Low-Country Christmas brunches, cocktail parties featuring martinis and Asian hors d'oeuvres, and tea parties for the elementary school set.

## Gift Cookbooks of All Kinds

Keepsake cookbooks designed and executed for a specific individual or group of individuals can be an amazing offering, guaranteed to bring ooohs, aaahs, and sometimes even a tear.

**FAST FACTS:** We can thank Pliny the Elder, a first-century Roman officer and naturalist, for much historical data about early agriculture, edible wild plants, and "exotic" trees. One of his works gives an extensive account of olive growing, types of olives, and olive oil production. He's also credited with writing about wild hops, which led Russian River Brewery to name an India Pale Ale (IPA) after him.

One year my daughter's elementary school class gave their teacher a cookbook on winter holiday sweets. Each two-page spread included a picture of one of the children in a holiday-themed frame, that child's recipe for a Christmas, Hanukkah, or New Year's Day dessert, and a quote from the child about the dish. On other pages we added holiday wishes, candid photos from classroom events, a title, and a dedication. The four-color pages were printed, bound in a heat-activated hard cover, and presented at the class holiday party. It was a huge success in which each child played a part.

Gift cookbooks can be prepared for one family member, as a tribute to his or her contribution to the family table or to commemorate a special anniversary. Or a mother might create a keepsake cookbook and distribute copies to all her children and grandchildren. One year my niece Erin gave my brother Colin a Father's Day gift of an elaborate, multicourse meal, beautifully served with the help of her siblings. She combined the menu, recipes for each dish, family photos, and a loving tribute to her dad into a lovely small cookbook as a remembrance of the occasion.

Office friends might combine farewell wishes with favorite recipes for a food-loving retiree's gift cookbook. Or, an extended family could collaborate on a gift cookbook for a child going off to college, moving into a first apartment, or moving across the country. Bridal showers that request a recipe from each guest—later compiled into a book with photos from the event—ensure that the bride and groom will have something to do with all those kitchen gadget gifts.

Small cookbooks—say, an individual cook's best bread recipes or pie collection, along with cooking tips and pithy sayings—can be produced in quantity to serve as party favors or small holiday gifts.

## You Can Do This!

A keepsake cookbook—whether created to be a grand feast or an intimate supper—is within reach of anyone who cares about food and his or her own culinary experiences. Before you begin collecting recipes, ask yourself these questions:

- What kind of cookbook interests you? Do you like a cookbook you can curl up with and read, or one with plenty of practical tips and fast facts?

- What foods really catch your interest? Are you all about chocolate? Or would you prefer to buy good chocolate and spend your kitchen time making gumbos and stews?

- Do most of your best dishes come from one branch of the family or one particular ethnic tradition? Are you a good cook, or just a really happy diner?

- Do you have a deadline—say, an anniversary or holiday—by which you'd like to have your keepsake cookbook completed?

- How much time are you willing to devote to your book? The product you can create spending an hour a day is appreciably different from the end result of spending a couple of hours a month.

- Do you prefer to work alone, or do you imagine sitting around a table with a group of friends or colleagues? If you expect to work with a group, what is your role?

- Who is the audience for your book? Is it just for you? For your children? Your supper club? Or everybody in your circle of friends and acquaintances?

- How technically savvy are you? Can you work with digital photos and recipes stored on a computer? Or do you literally cut and paste your memories into scrapbooks?

- What special interests do you or your collaborators have that might add to the book? Are you a photographer, an artist, a collector, or a writer? Or do you and your friends share quality time over your daughters' Girl Scout troop or church charity drives?

Mull over the questions, write down the answers, and walk away for a day. Then come back and consider your options. If you love beautifully detailed gourmet cookbooks, have some digital photography skills, and want to create a work of art featuring your own recipes, you'll need to plan a long-term timeline for this labor of love. Your incentive is knowing it will be fabulous when it's done. On the other hand, a kitschy, fun cookbook full of family photos, funny sayings, kids' drawings, and birthday cake recipes might be just as satisfying and a lot less time-consuming. A heritage cookbook that involves drawing family history and cooking techniques from far-flung relatives can be an intense, gratifying six-month project or a well-paced, multistage effort that goes on for a year or two. Of course, any cookbook project that involves more than one author will require agreement on the book scope and theme, as well as a cooperative timeline and a division of labor.

In upcoming chapters, we'll talk about how to plot, organize, and assemble your keepsake cookbook. You'll also find boxes with snippets of food history, food lore, and cooking tips sprinkled throughout this book. Feel free to use these fast facts in your cookbook to fill out a page or add another dimension to the text. Or you can use the ideas to model your own fast facts!

# Getting Started: What You'll Need

Your cookbook is going to be fabulous. It's going to be a labor of love. It's going to be a unique expression of your culinary heritage or experience, and that of your collaborators if you're working in a group. All you need to make it happen is a plan and a few tools.

This chapter puts all the aspects of creating a cookbook on the table, so to speak, so you can see that your book is not only possible, but eminently doable.

Let's start with the plan. If you answered the questions at the end of the last chapter, you should be well on your way to creating the blueprint for your keepsake cookbook. You know what you want, who will be involved, and how much time you have to devote to the project. Next you'll make a very basic outline to guide your movements and ensure that everything stays on track.

## Creating Your Blueprint

### Step One: State Your Intentions

Look over your answers to the questions in Chapter 1 and write a simple, concise paragraph telling what you hope to capture with your book, who your audience will be, and how you plan to reach that audience. Remember, a cookbook geared toward your children, nieces, and nephews would have a different look and feel than one aimed at gardening enthusiasts or members of your service organization.

Be precise:

• I am creating a family heirloom. This book will be shared with extended family members and will include stories, scanned documents, and pictures from our grandparents' and parents' lives. It will capture their everyday and holiday recipes.

• I am creating a cookbook to appeal to dog lovers to raise money for my rescue group. The book will include stories and "glamour shots" of adopted rescue dogs. In addition, the book will have recipes from our group's monthly potluck dinners.

- I am creating a favorite desserts cookbook to give as wedding gifts to my friends' children. The book will have twenty-four recipes and pictures of my best homemade sweets, with tips on baking and candy making. I'll include quotes from famous people about living a "sweet life."

- My sister and I are creating a cookbook based on our years in the catering business. We want to share recipes but also to share what we've learned about entertaining and feeding large and small crowds.

State whether your book will be a traditional printed cookbook, a digital cookbook, or a web page, or whether you plan to start with a digital book and consider printing options later. Maybe you're considering something unusual, like a photo calendar with recipes. Whatever your vision, write it down. And don't worry about writing style or tone—this is strictly a utilitarian exercise.

## Step Two: Define the Scope of Your Book

Is this book limited to recipes from a particular holiday, a particular branch of your family, or a particular culinary genre or geographic area? Who are the contributors? How big do you expect this cookbook to be, and how much time do you expect to devote to it? Answer these questions in a short paragraph or an annotated list, and you'll have a good idea of the size of your project. For example:

- I want to write a holiday cookie cookbook. I'll include all the recipes I've used to make treats for my daughters' classes and clubs. I'll also include those I used for my own Christmas cookie jar and for gifts. Including bar cookies, I expect I'll have about sixty recipes. Since the recipes have already been tested, I should be able to work on the book for a few hours a week and have recipes, tips, and comments written within two months.

- My cookbook will include all the recipes of my Oklahoma-born grandmother and great-grandmother, who came to the San Joaquin Valley of California when their family fled the Dust Bowl. I expect to collect more than 200 recipes. I also plan to include stories about the family during the Dust Bowl and how they became Californians, so this cookbook will take six to eight months.

- Our women's club cookbook will chronicle twenty-five years of our "jazz brunch" events to benefit the college jazz program. The book will have mementos, bios, and about 125 recipes. We'll divide the recipes into fruits and salads, eggs and savory entrees, side dishes, breakfast breads and pancakes, and sweets. Information will come from the club archives and the recipes will come from the chefs/restaurants that contributed the food. The cookbook committee will test the recipes for home use. The book has to be ready to print in five months so we can give copies to the twenty-fifth anniversary brunch sponsors.

Getting this information on paper allows you to envision the book that's living in your subconscious mind. Once you define the scope of your cookbook, you'll be in a better position to plan the time and work involved. *The Twelve Desserts of Christmas* and *The Miller Family Pennsylvania Dutch Feast Book* are both great keepsake cookbooks and both within your grasp. One will just take a bit more effort than the other!

## Step Three: Identify Your Elements

Since this is a cookbook, we'll assume that you want to include recipes. But what else should be part of the mix? Do you want vignettes and essays about events and places from your childhood? Do you want first-person stories from elderly family members or senior members of your organization? Do you want to include cooking tips from a variety of people? Charts? Bits of historical data? Short profiles?

**FAST FACTS:** Need a substitute for buttermilk? Mix 1 cup fresh milk with 1 tablespoon white vinegar. Let stand 3 to 5 minutes and use in place of buttermilk in recipes.

How do you plan to illustrate your book? You can use food photos, vintage photos, contemporary photos, original artwork, family tree segments, travel postcards, scanned documents and memorabilia, decorative borders and stickers, and vintage documents. Are you an artist or photographer, or will your illustrations have a craft-centered or homey feel?

For my memoir cookbook *Roux Memories: A Cajun-Creole Love Story with Recipes*, the "elements" paragraph would look like this:

*Book will include authentic Cajun and Creole recipes from both sides of the family, stories about what we ate and why, biographical notes about different family members, essays about growing up in South Louisiana, recipe notes to explain ingredients and techniques, funny sayings, vintage family photos, a few food photos.*

The tenth anniversary cookbook for your neighborhood's annual sweet-and-savory pie sale to support the local playground might have this elements paragraph:

*We will have recipes from each family that participates in the sale, totaling 120 recipes, including appetizer tarts, dessert tarts, savory pies, fruit pies, cream pies, and other sweet pies. Front essay should tell the history of the sale and the involvement with the playground. Each section includes pictures of tarts or pies, and some pictures taken at the sale tables. Add photos from the playground scrapbook showing the annual improvements and a description of what was done. Also, pictures of children playing on the equipment.*

The women's club twenty-fifth anniversary jazz brunch cookbook referenced in the previous section would have the following elements paragraph:

*Include recipes from participating chefs with pictures and short bios of each, menus from each year, photos of scholarship presentations, photos of the jazz band, photos from the annual brunch events, bios of scholarship recipients. Need statement from this year's club chair, statement from head of the college jazz program.*

### Step Four: Identify Your Sources and Resources

Where will you get the elements to build your cookbook? Who has the recipes? Will you be able to get written recipes, or will you have to coax them from the memories of family and friends? How many recipes already reside in your own brain or recipe box? If your cookbook is going to be a cooperative venture, are you each bringing recipes to the collective pot? Or are you planning a division of labor where some participants harvest recipes, others design pages, and still others edit the finished product?

How will you handle photos? Will you have to travel with your photo scanner and laptop in a suitcase? Are your relatives and friends likely to send digital copies or hard copies of photos for the project? If you plan to use food photos, are you going to do the styling? Or will you ask relatives to take pictures of family dinners and gatherings? If your cookbook celebrates an organization or region, will you be able to tap existing archives or call on contacts to share their photo albums?

What stories or anecdotes can you write from your own memory? Who should you or your collaborators interview for more anecdotes or to enhance the stories you've already identified? For example:

- The Hulin Sisters Cookbook: On hand, 135 written recipes; need at least 100 more. Angela will collect recipes we don't have by sitting with Mom and going through our "wish list." If a large number of recipes have to be prepared, we will all pitch in to buy groceries. Erin and Lauren will test recipes with help from Sophie and Brenda. Monica will collect and scan vintage family photos from Mom's and siblings' albums. She will get the identities of those in the old pictures from Mom and Aunt Lillian. Belinda will write short biographies of our parents, grandparents on both sides, and aunts and uncles on both sides. She will attempt to get a funny or interesting anecdote about each one by talking to Mom and by calling/e-mailing our cousins.

- The Riverside Save-a-Sheltie Benefit Cookbook: Each of five committee members will be responsible for collecting, editing, and entering the recipes for one segment (appetizers, soups, salads, entrees, desserts) of the book. Photos and rescue stories will come from members who have adopted Shelties; Darla and Sam will collect and edit. Fran and Joe will organize material in sections in a digital file. Ray will design camera-ready pages.

- The Gator Tail-Gator Cookbook: Each tailgate co-op family is responsible for producing three complete tailgate party menus, with recipes and digital photos from the events. Jeannie will edit and organize the menus and recipes. Mark will write copy about the history of the group, the purpose of the cookbook, and the families involved. Donna will collect statistics from the football seasons. Bob will create the e-book pages and upload the book to our website.

## Step Five: Decide On a Format

Your keepsake cookbook can take the form of a professionally bound book with color illustrations and elegant design. It can be a digital e-book that you distribute over the Internet. It can be a small gift book or a full-size scrapbook. You can even build your cookbook as an interactive website if you like.

Deciding how you want the finished product to look, and how it will be distributed, is a critical piece of the keepsake cookbook puzzle. You may be able to create your cookbook manually, scan the pages (or have them scanned), and then have the digital files printed at a quick-print shop. You can work with a cookbook printing company or a print-on-demand publisher. Or you can produce the entire project yourself, using design software and simple binding equipment.

**FAST FACTS:** Can't imagine your favorite pizza without tomato sauce? Well, you can thank Columbus. Italians didn't start eating tomatoes until the 1500s, after the great explorer brought them from the New World.

What you can accomplish in the way of production values depends largely on the talents and means of you, your friends, and your collaborators. If your group includes photographers, designers, and web mavens, a professional-quality keepsake cookbook is easily within your reach. If you have to purchase such services, you may want to consider an attractive but simpler presentation.

State your loftiest goal and, if it will keep you from getting discouraged, a secondary goal. For example:

- I want to write a family heritage cookbook with color photos of each dish, professionally printed and bound, suitable for selling through bookstores. (Interim step: A family cookbook designed by me and bound using home equipment or quick-print services, suitable for gifting to family members.)

- We want to build an interactive recipe website that Historical Society members can contribute to and download from, with illustrations and historical pedigree of each dish offered in some detail. (Interim step: We will prepare an e-cookbook that can be e-mailed to members and sold to nonmembers. It will cover dining in the Victorian era in Springfield.)

- I want to create a small, professionally printed Christmas cookie cookbook illustrated with original holiday-themed drawings from my grandchildren, along with Christmas wishes and sayings. (Interim step: I will print and bind twelve copies at home to distribute to the grandchildren on Christmas Eve.)

### Step Six: Build a Timeline

Now get out a calendar. Pick a target date for your completed book. Then set deadlines for every week between now and then. The stages of your individual book might vary, but in general, consider these your main tasks:

- Collecting recipes

- Collecting stories and anecdotes

- Testing recipes

- Taking photographs

- Collecting existing photographs

- Collecting art elements

- Preparing recipes for publication

- Editing narratives

- Designing cookbook pages

- Assembling the cookbook

**FAST FACTS:** Not sure if that can of baking powder is still active? Drop ¼ teaspoon of baking powder in a tablespoon of water. If it foams, it's good. If not, toss it.

Depending on the size of your project and the number of people involved, it could take three or more weeks to complete each stage. The important thing is to keep the momentum going by making weekly progress.

## Your Blueprint

Once you've gone through the steps to create your blueprint, you should have enough information to create a production plan that looks something like this:

## Blueprint Example 1

### *Hulin Family Cookbook*

| Step One: Intentions | I am creating a Cajun-Creole heritage cookbook starring my extended family. The book is for my family, as well as all the South Louisiana families who need written recipes for the dishes they love. I especially want to help people who lost recipes during Hurricanes Katrina and Rita. |
|---|---|
| Step Two: Scope | Recipes from all branches of the family, including re-created oral recipes from grandparents. The book will have ten chapters and at least 250 authentic recipes reflecting the Cajun-Creole table through the lens of one family tree. |
| Step Three: Elements | My book will include recipes, vintage family photographs, essays and recollections, family sayings, and recipe notes explaining when and why we ate some of the dishes in the book. |
| Step Four: Sources and Resources | I have most of the written recipes in my possession. For oral recipes, I will interview my mother and cousins. I will ask for my mother's help in re-creating "lost" recipes. Photos will come from my albums and those of my siblings and my mother. I will write the essays and recollections. |
| Step Five: Format | This book will be produced in a digital format, using standardized recipe formats, text boxes, and scanned photographs. Presentation software will be used for templates. Once created, the book will be saved as a PDF file and printed in limited runs as needed. |
| Step Six: Timeline | The process should take six months from start to finished digital work. **Week 1:** Send e-mails to family members, telling them what I'm doing and asking for any stories, recipes, and photos they'd like to share. **Weeks 2–8:** Gather, test, and type recipes in my possession. Write recipe notes with each recipe. Begin to scan my photos into the computer. **Weeks 9–12:** Collect or re-create recipes not in my possession. Type recipes in proper recipe format and add recipe notes. Review photos in Mom's and siblings' albums. Scan selected pictures. **Weeks 13–15:** Finish scanning photos. Add captions. **Weeks 16–20:** Write essays, sayings, and any additional prose content. **Weeks 21–24:** Create book by using templates to combine elements and lay out recipes, text, and photos. **Weeks 25–26:** Copyedit material carefully, save cookbook as a PDF file, and consider printing options. |

# Blueprint Example 2

## *The Gabby Gourmet Club Cookbook*

| Step One: Intentions | We are creating a cookbook to document ten years of fun and dining at one another's homes. The book is for our families, as well as for others who want to start successful gourmet clubs. We'd also like to sell copies to benefit the local food bank. |
|---|---|
| Step Two: Scope | We meet six times a year for sit-down dinners, plus a New Year's Eve finger-foods potluck. We will pick the twenty-five best recipes in ten categories—finger foods, appetizers, soups, salads, pasta dishes, entrees, vegetables and starches, desserts, and libations—for 250 recipes. |
| Step Three: Elements | The book will include recipes, menus, photos from our dinners, a history of the group, tips on how to organize a gourmet club, recipe notes, and funny things "overheard" at our dinner parties. |
| Step Four: Sources and Resources | Each couple who hosts a dinner is responsible for producing a printed menu for the evening. We will use the menus to vote on the best dishes. The person who brought the dish will be responsible for contributing the recipe and recipe notes. Photos will come from the shared album we keep. The tips will be contributed by Alice and Jean. Everyone will contribute funny quotes and remembrances. |
| Step Five: Format | This book will be produced in a digital format, using standardized recipe formats, text boxes, and scanned photographs and menus. John will lay out the pages in InDesign. Once created, the book will be shared digitally among club members. Dora will shop printers or publishers for a full print run after we arrange distribution through stores and restaurants that support the food bank. |
| Step Six: Timeline | Six months from start to finished digital work.<br>**Week 1:** Collect menus. Send e-mails to members to schedule a time to vote on recipes.<br>**Weeks 2–9:** Decide on recipe list. Collect recipes in correct format and recipe notes from each member. Collect tips from Alice and Jean. Dora will edit.<br>**Weeks 10–12:** Meet to look at photo album to select usable pictures. Scan pictures or collect digital versions from the person who shot the photo. Scan menus.<br>**Weeks 13–15:** At dinner meeting, write captions for the photos. Brainstorm for favorite quotes. Decide who will write up quotes and send to Dora for edit.<br>**Weeks 16–20:** Clean up odds and ends. Begin turning edited sections over to John for layout.<br>**Weeks 21–24:** John completes layout and cover design. Dora gives report on printer/publisher research.<br>**Weeks 25–26:** Final review by each group member. Save cookbook as a PDF file and distribute to group members. Get a few books printed to shop to retailers to assess interest. |

Once your cookbook production effort gets under way, you may want to create a separate, more-detailed timeline. This will be particularly helpful if you have several people working on the project. You can build a timeline that indicates deliverables from each person involved.

Now that you know the general steps involved in creating your book, we can move on to some of the specific actions you'll need to take to flesh out your keepsake.

## Tools and Techniques—Digital

Here's a wonderful secret: Basic computer software—the office package you likely have installed on your Mac or PC right this second—offers almost everything you need to put together a perfectly acceptable cookbook, complete with photos or artwork, recipes, essays, and recipe notes or tips. The only additional tools required are a scanner and a color printer.

In the coming chapters, we'll discuss tips for collecting recipes and writing them like a pro, as well as the best methods for gathering and using art elements. But for now, we're simply talking logistics. Here's how to handle the information you have, and how to record and compile the information you're going get.

To get started, just start typing.

1. Create a document folder called Family Cookbook or use your project's actual title. Add subfolders called Blueprint, Recipes, Stories, and Fillers. In your pictures directory, create a Cookbook folder, with subfolders for Photographs and Art Scans. (Or use your favorite picture management software to subdivide art elements.)

2. Save your blueprint document, other planning materials, and ideas in the Blueprint subfolder. In the Recipes subfolder, make a separate document file for each recipe that you enter or cut-and-paste from e-mailed or previously stored recipes. Name each file with a standard naming convention, using the recipe name and a code number for the title. The codes should be simple—1 for appetizers, 2 for soups, 3 for chicken dishes, 4 for beef, and so on. You may decide to move dishes into different categories for the actual book, but in the meantime, the number codes will help you search and locate specific groups of recipes. So,

the file name for your aunt's tea cookies might be Berthasteacookies_8 .doc. Fill the Stories subfolder with essays, interviews, anecdotes, and research—all clearly labeled for easy searching. For example, the Stories directory might include snowdaysessay.doc, familyvacayanecdote.doc, and grannyinterview1.doc.

3. In your pictures directory, use the Photographs subfolder to hold digital pictures that you copy from your existing digital collection or that friends and collaborators e-mail to you, as well as high-resolution scans of hard-copy photos. In the Art Scans subfolder, store scans of handwritten recipes, ticket stubs, postcards, maps, family trees, and other elements you can use in your layout. Remember that downloaded or scanned photos will be loaded into your computer with an identifier code of letters and numbers. You'll want to save the pictures with names that mean something to you.

Now, to create a lovely, easy-to-manage family or group cookbook, load Power-Point or another presentation program into your computer. Select a layout with two boxes on the page, preferably with one slightly larger than the other. A side-by-side layout usually works best. Use the upload or cut-and-paste feature to insert an ingredients list and an instructions section to the boxes on the page.

On the next slide, upload a photo and a note, or a full-page photo, pull-out quote, essay, recipe note, or scanned art element. You can select a template that offers the boxes you wish to use, or pick a blank slide you can fill as you wish.

These slides can be rearranged as needed and will become facing pages in your cookbook. Generally, it helps to keep the recipe slides consistently configured, with the same ingredient-instruction positioning throughout. The art or essay-intensive slides can have two or three different formats, depending on the number of elements on the page. Try to achieve some uniformity in the pages—don't overcrowd one page while leaving a lot of white space on another.

**FAST FACTS:** Need a quick-fix vegetable soup? Use a large jar or can of inexpensive prepared spaghetti sauce, plus two cans of beef broth and water to taste. Add whatever fresh or frozen veggies you have on hand and a bit of smoked sausage or leftover pot roast. Simmer 20 to 30 minutes.

Add title slides, with or without art, for the book cover and for section dividers. The slides—actually pages—can be printed by you, uploaded to a website, e-mailed, or downloaded to a flash drive for sharing or printing elsewhere. You can save presentations as PDF files, which may make printing and sharing easier.

**FAST FACTS:** Did you know that nonfat evaporated milk can be whipped into an emulsion similar to heavy cream? While you won't get the flavor of cream, the texture can help lighten whipped or frozen desserts without adding a lot of saturated fat. The secret is to get the evaporated milk, bowl, and beaters really cold first.

If you or one of your collaborators has more sophisticated design skills, a desktop publishing product like Adobe InDesign, Microsoft Publisher, or QuarkXPress can be pressed into service to create printer-ready pages.

Hobbyists who enjoy working with digital scrapbooking software will find most of the commercially available programs adaptable to creating a keepsake cookbook. Digital scrapbooking programs by Nova Development, Hallmark, StoryRock, Serif, Ltd., and others cost $20 to $50. They include a broad range of backgrounds, borders, themes, cutouts, and layout options. The downside of these programs is that they take up a large amount of memory on your computer. Also, designs and flourishes too liberally applied can make your cookbook look amateurish and busy, rather than clean and compelling.

Cookbook- and recipe-creation software exists in the $20 to $80 price range, with more expensive versions for nutritionists and dietitians. The chief advantage of these programs lies in the database functions they offer. Most include a large library of recipes as well as nutritional data, shopping list generation, and sophisticated sorting functions. Some have good layout options for personal recipe pages, but in general, these programs are designed to create comprehensive digital cookbooks.

## Tools and Techniques—the Low-Tech Option

If you've ever created a scrapbook or photo album, you can produce a keepsake cookbook partly or completely by hand. You'll need some way of producing typed or printed recipes for clarity, but otherwise, you can build each page as a labor of love.

Use a file box with folders, or buy a large accordion folder to organize the material you collect. Make separate folders for recipes, notes and stories, photos, mementos, and other art elements. Color-code the folders to make it easy to identify different types of elements. This is particularly helpful if you need more than one folder to handle your photos, or if you want to divide the recipes into categories based on ingredient, course, era, or author.

Decide how you want to present the recipes in your book—for example, in the traditional format of a dinner menu with appetizers, soups and salads, entrees, side dishes, breads, and desserts, or in some other order. If you're producing a travelogue cookbook, you may want to arrange the recipes based on the location or the year of the trip. Holiday cookbooks can be menu-driven, ingredient-driven, or built around a timeline.

Once you decide how to present the recipes, gather the materials that will augment each recipe—photos, notes, memorabilia—then go to work.

Select a standard-size scrapbook album or an attractive binder filled with page protectors. Select presentation-weight paper sheets in the colors or patterns you desire. (You'll find a huge selection at your local crafts store.) Use decorative-edge scissors, borders, contrasting-color mats, and stickers to trim and augment printed recipes, recipe instructions, stories, photos, and notes. With a glue stick, glue dots, or double-sided tape, secure recipes and mementos onto pages and carefully load the pages into page protectors.

Scrapbookers tend to fall into two camps, the less-is-more group and the more-is-more group. This is your cookbook, and if you can't imagine a page that isn't adorned with rickrack borders, paper hearts, and stickers, by all means have at it. But do remember that you're creating a cookbook that you want people to use. Try to be consistent with the placement and layout of the recipe pages. Make sure adornments don't block or squeeze recipe ingredients or instructions.

Do attempt to limit your color choices to a palette of three main hues, and always use solid colors to frame, back, or mat color photos. If you plan to copy the finished pages, use a color scheme that provides enough contrast among the elements.

**FAST FACTS:** Allow your late-season herbs to blossom and you'll have tasty flowers to garnish your salads and entrees. Purple chive and pink thyme blossoms, yellow dill and white basil flowers, can be tossed with mixed lettuces, squash blossoms, nasturtiums, and fresh lavender into a colorful salad.

Once all the cookbook pages have been created and loaded into a binder or album, you can enjoy your beautiful handmade keepsake. Or you can share the joy. Each page of your cookbook can be scanned, either by you or at a quick-print shop, and turned into a digital file. Those files can then be copied onto disks for gifts, printed and bound, or printed and loaded into scrapbooks.

## Getting Down to the Details

In the next chapter, we'll get to the heart of every keepsake cookbook—the recipes. We'll talk about collecting written and unwritten recipes, plus re-creating all those recipes you may consider lost. Your keepsake cookbook project will bring them back to life.

# Collecting Recipes: Uncovering Written and Unwritten Treasures

Some family and heirloom recipes have been written down and carefully filed. Many have not. As with the legends that wind through a family tree, culinary traditions often exist orally, passing from one generation, one cook, to the next in an extended ritual of bonding. It's a beautiful thing—until there's a break in the line. Then we have Cousin Jean frantically e-mailing and calling relatives near and far to track down Granny's Moravian gingersnaps recipe, which may or may not have been shared.

Still other recipes are written in such cryptic or vernacular fashion as to be useless to anyone other than the recipe author and his or her immediate minions. (Do you know what your great-uncle really meant when he directed future cooks to spit-roast a "goodly haunch" of venison over a "half measure" of coals?) Or maybe a clearly written recipe for a favorite dessert exists—you know it came off a box of cake mix—if only you could remember what the dessert was called.

These challenges can be daunting, but they're also likely to be the very things that drove you to write a keepsake cookbook. Collecting and clarifying those culinary instructions can solve generations-old kitchen mysteries and give modern cooks a gift from the past.

If you come from a family of fastidious record keepers who wrote down each and every pot roast, crumpet, and cake recipe served, or if you belong to a group that frequently shares written recipes, consider yourself lucky. You can gather the recipes and move on to the next chapter, which deals with writing recipes properly. Otherwise, gather 'round. We're going to address the task of collecting recipes for your keepsake cookbook.

## Collecting and Clarifying Written Recipes

In the last chapter, you identified the person or persons who have the recipes you want for your cookbook. Now it's time to contact them. The simplest way to handle recipe collection for this type of cookbook is face-to-face, over tea or coffee or a glass of wine. Unless the cookbook is going to be a surprise, call or e-mail and explain what you're doing and why you'd like to peruse your friend's, relative's, or associate's recipe box. Make this initial approach friendly, fun, and low-pressure; chances are you'll be back again to discuss unwritten recipes, family or organization history, and legends. You don't want your initial burst of enthusiasm to scare off your sources!

If your recipe source isn't local, you'll have to stage virtual encounters through extended e-mails, phone calls, or even regular mail.

Now, be prepared. You'll likely encounter one of two reactions when you share your plans. First, your source may embrace your keepsake cookbook project as enthusiastically as if it were his or her own. He or she will get busy, gathering together recipes as well as suggesting other sources for material. Understand that at some level, your relative or friend may feel that you've relieved them of a looming obligation. If *you're* going to write the family or garden club cookbook, they don't have to! Of course, that doesn't mean they will refrain from giving you the full force of their opinions on what you should or should not include in your book. And that's just fine. Listen politely, gather the material you need, and proceed according to your plan.

The second most common reaction is reluctance. A few people—not many in my experience—feel very possessive of their recipes and do not want to share. However, most reluctant sources aren't guilty of recipe hoarding. They simply lack confidence in the quality of their recipe files, the neatness of their collection, or in their ability to help. ("I just make it the way I always have . . . it's nothing fancy.") In this case, you'll need to be reassuring and patient, and ready to be effusive over any crumbs that come your way. Once these relatives or friends realizes that they are being helpful, chances are they'll continue to pull more recipes from boxes, books, and drawers.

Interestingly, I encountered both types of reaction when I was writing my memoir cookbook *Roux Memories*. But once the book was done and everyone could see what I'd been trying to accomplish, the floodgates opened. Happily, I now have more stories, more photos, and more recipes than I could have fit into the first book, and maybe enough to begin another book!

The old-school method of recipe sharing—namely, sitting there and copying each recipe by hand onto a recipe card or notebook page—is too tedious for more than a few dishes. Instead, borrow the recipes long enough to dart into a print shop with self-serve copiers. Spend a few dollars and copy the entire batch, being careful to check contrast levels so the recipes can be read. Then, you can type them into the correct format and add them to your cookbook at your leisure. Be sure to return the originals!

Another option is to bring a document-quality scanner along to tea and scan the recipes directly to a laptop computer, flash drive, or other digital storage medium. If your recipe source is computer-savvy and willing to assist, you may be able to get him or her to scan the recipes and e-mail them to you, or load them onto a portable flash drive that you provide. This is particularly helpful when collecting recipes long-distance.

**FAST FACTS:** Cranberries, an American native fruit, contain nutrients and chemical compounds that have been shown to fight coronary artery disease, urinary tract infections, and some types of cancer. Use the ultra-tart berries in place of vinegar or lemon juice to brighten savory dishes.

The important thing is to make sure you understand the recipes you collect. Review the written instructions and get your source to clarify anything you don't understand as soon as you get the recipe. If the recipe is an heirloom that neither you nor the source has prepared, try to come to a consensus about any handwriting flourishes, unusual terms, or notations. It will make life easier when you begin testing recipes.

## Collecting Unwritten Recipes

As we've discussed, many recipes are part of an oral tradition, handed from one cook to the next. But just because a recipe hasn't been written down, doesn't mean it can't be.

My maternal grandmother's beef *boulettes,* my Aunt Rose's chopped salad, and my mother's eggplant casserole were all unwritten recipes when I began collecting. Only my mother was still available to walk me through the process. The beef *boulettes* were a distant memory for me but a well-loved dish from my mother's childhood. Mom and I talked about the dish—the texture, the seasoning, the size of the *boulettes,* the sauce—and I made several versions until one recipe seemed just right. As for Aunt Rose's salad, I remembered sitting at her kitchen table, talking to her and watching her make the salad. Her salad represented the first time in my life I'd ever tasted avocados, a key ingredient in her salads, and the memory was seared in my brain. Although I was able to re-create the salad and the homemade dressing, I really couldn't figure out how—at that time in Lafayette, Louisiana—my aunt was able to have such an abundance of avocados. After my cookbook appeared, my cousin Brenda explained. It seems their neighbor had a wonderfully prolific avocado bush in the backyard and she shared the harvest! My aunt was one of the few people in the neighborhood who loved avocados.

Coaxing a recipe from a family member, friend, or noted kitchen maven could be as simple as watching the cook prepare the dish and taking notes. For more hands-on research, keep an assortment of clean bowls and measuring utensils on hand. When your recipe author/cook begins to add ingredients, interrupt the process to define quantities. Use a bowl to catch that "lump" of butter that's about to be added to a pan. Measure it with a measuring spoon or cup, and note whether the butter is cold, softened, whipped, salted, or unsalted. Then follow through as the butter gets added to the pan and note whether it is cooked until browned, melted, or combined with other ingredients.

You can follow the same process with oil, flour, seasonings, and other ingredients. Meats, seafood, and tubers can be quantified by noting the weight of the package before cooking. Be sure to note whether onions and other aromatic vegetables are sautéed until browned before adding other ingredients, or if they're just wilted, or if they're thrown into an already simmering pot of broth. Are meats lightly browned in oil before adding broth, or are cuts browned until crusty? Are seasonings rubbed in or just sprinkled on? Little details like these will affect both the flavor and texture of the dish.

**FAST FACTS:** Your grandmother's cast iron pots stayed rust-free for one reason: She never washed the pots with detergent. A cast iron pot seasoned with oil or shortening and heated gradually will cook foods evenly with delicious results. Clean the pot with hot water and a nylon or natural-bristle brush. Dry thoroughly.

Sometimes it's helpful to interview the cook before any kitchen action takes place. Ask where he or she learned to prepare the dish. Did it come from a long-ago neighbor or friend? Or was the dish part of the family repertoire when the cook was growing up? If so, is the current version different from the original? In many cases, you'll learn that the cook you're interviewing adapted the dish to modern ingredients or tastes, using lean chicken breasts instead of a whole chicken, reducing the amount of salt and adding other seasonings, or turning a mutton dish into a beef dish. Although you want to capture the version of the recipe you remember, it's helpful to know the history of the dish. You can add that information in a note in your book, or you can use it to learn more about some of the transitions your family or your friends made.

Ask the cook how long it takes to prepare the dish, what the predominant flavors should be, and what parts of the cooking process are critical. Some entrees cook over low heat for hours without attention, and then, at the end of cooking or with the addition of new ingredients, must be nurtured and stirred constantly. If there's dough involved, is it yeast-raised or leavened with baking powder or simply a shortening-rich pastry? Are animal proteins browned in oil on the stove, or slowly browned in an oven? Is the sauce thickened with flour or cornstarch, strained, or served *au jus*?

If you can lean on your friend or relative a little more, try making the dish yourself, according to the instructions you gathered. Have the recipe originator taste the dish and recommend adjustments.

## Re-creating "Lost" Recipes

As long as someone alive can remember how a dish smells, looks, and tastes, the dish isn't lost. Your late grandfather's sweet-and-sour pot roast is, at its core, a pot roast—a dish with only a few classic cooking methods. The variables include the cut of meat used, the sweetening agent, the acidic agent, the seasonings, the browning method (if any), and the length of time in the oven, on the stove, or in the slow cooker. It may take you several trial runs and a few phone conversations with cousins to get the recipe just right, but it absolutely is possible.

Begin re-creating a lost recipe with a little research:

- Write down what you remember, or what you've been told, about the dish. Call relatives or friends who might be familiar with the dish and ask for their memories of it, the cooking process, the occasions when it was served, if it was seasonal, and any sensory details they can recall—smells, texture, temperature.

- Examine the name of the dish with an open mind. For example, a dish with the name "peas" in it could refer to fresh green peas or to a thick porridge of dried split peas. It could refer to black-eyed or crowder peas. It could also refer to the West Indian staple, rice and pigeon peas. When I was growing up, my Cajun grandmother frequently made a plain, single-layer cake for an afternoon snack. She called it *mâche-pain,* which I thought must have been some sort of corruption of the word *marzipan*—a treat that would have been hard to come by in rural Louisiana. After a little more research, I realized it's a corruption of the French expression for "make plain" and the batter for it tastes very similar to madeleine cakes. Interestingly, madeleines are a specialty of the Lorraine region of France, where many of my grandmother's ancestors lived.

- Consider the dish originator's ethnic background. For example, cabbage rolls or stuffed cabbage can be found in many European and Middle Eastern family repertoires. Eastern European cooks generally make beef- or lamb-stuffed cabbage rolls in a sweet-and-sour tomato-based sauce. In some parts of Europe, large pickled cabbage leaves may be stuffed with seasoned bulgur wheat, while in Scandinavia, cabbage rolls are sauced with thinned lingonberry preserves. Acadian cooks in South Louisiana make spicy cabbage rolls stuffed with beef and rice, baked in a garlic-laced tomato sauce. If you know the ethnic origins of a dish, or the ethnic influences on the cook, you'll have an easier time deciding whether to add a little brown sugar, fruit juice, vinegar, or tomato to the evolving recipe.

- Review cookbooks and recipe websites for similar dishes. Look at recipes that have the same ethnic origins as your relative or friend, as well as recipes from the late cook's final geographic region. An Irish cook with a fabulous mutton stew recipe may have allowed that recipe to evolve into a venison stew after moving to central Pennsylvania, where hunting is a favorite pastime and deer are plentiful. Likewise, a raspberry-topped custard tart first made in New England could have become a delicious blackberry or strawberry pie when the cook's family moved to Florida.

**FAST FACTS:** Commercially prepared chili powder is actually a spice blend that includes powdered dried chiles, cumin, garlic powder, oregano, and salt. Buy individual spices and make your own signature blend.

- Finally, consider the era of the recipe. You may never perfectly re-create the flaky tenderness of your great aunt's meat pie pastry if you're unwilling to use chilled lard in the crust. To capture the vibrant color and flavor of your mother's homemade strawberry jam, you'll have to buy sun-ripened, just-picked strawberries—possibly an heirloom variety—rather than the hard, cotton-centered berries found in many supermarkets.

## The Role of Ethnicity in Family Food History

Perhaps you live in an enclave where the culinary past clearly shines through in contemporary menus. That makes you both lucky and unusual. Most likely you're part of the global culinary melting pot, where your Chinese-style stir-fry is made with Japanese soy sauce, leftover New Zealand lamb, and Chilean vegetables cooked in a flat-bottom wok made in the United States. Certainly, being part of that global exchange has advantages. But it can make it more difficult to re-create the exact flavors of lost vintage recipes.

If you're struggling with the spices, ingredients, and cooking techniques in a dish, consider some of these general characteristics of some popular ethnic fare. This list isn't meant to chronicle the cuisines of the world, but to give you a few variables to consider when re-creating a recipe.

## Armenia

Lamb, freshwater fish, cracked wheat, thick yogurt, flatbreads, eggplant, cumin, caraway seeds, sesame seeds and paste, grape leaves, peppers, and tomatoes are all used extensively in Armenian cuisine. But one of the things that best characterizes this cooking style is a love of stuffed dishes. Cabbage leaves, grape leaves, fish, large cuts of meat, vegetables like zucchini and onions, fruits, and even meatballs are often stuffed with pasty mixtures of cracked wheat, finely ground meat, vegetables, seeds, and nuts. Savory stews may include dried apricots, quince, or other fruits. Unusual or out-of-the-ordinary flavorings include rose water, orange water, powdered sumac, and *mahlav*. Phyllo dough appears in sweets and pastries.

## China

Food historians have identified eight distinctive regional cuisines in China, and many of the cooking traditions in each region date back more than 5,000 years. It's difficult to duplicate "Chinese cooking" because the canvas is so vast, but also because ingredients and lifestyle factors change (some subtly, some more dramatically) the farther you get from the home country. Early Chinese settlers in North America learned to prepare dishes that resembled those from home but used locally available ingredients. As a result, home cooking to some third- and fourth-generation Chinese Americans includes sautéed American broccoli instead of the long, leafy broccoli of mainland China, as well as more animal proteins.

**FAST FACTS:** For quick mocha brownies, use cold strong coffee instead of water in your favorite brownie mix.

At the same time, commercially prepared Chinese sauces—which are widely used throughout the Far East—have become much more readily available in other parts of the world, giving modern cookbook writers a chance at capturing Chinese flavors more clearly. Peruse any large supermarket's ethnic foods aisle and you'll find a full range of soy sauces, hoisin sauce, duck sauce, hot mustard, fermented black beans, oyster sauce, hot chili sauce, and any number of sauce blends.

The important thing to remember when writing recipes for Chinese dishes is this: The secret is in the preparation. More so than other traditions, Chinese cooking relies on ingredients being carefully selected, cut in uniform shapes and sizes, and marinated as needed before cooking begins. The cooking process, which often begins with hot oil or a steaming rack, is a relatively simple matter once the preparation has taken place.

## England

Traditional English cuisine—the cooking traditions immigrants brought to other countries, and the core of much American cooking—tends to be straightforward and uncomplicated. The "Sunday dinner" of roasted meat, potatoes, and gravy is an English custom, and while the meat could be beef, lamb, pork, or fowl, the best English cooks always brought a bronze, well-caramelized, juicy cut or bird to the table. If you're trying to recapture the Sunday after-church pot roast or chicken made by your grandma in Atlanta, you'd do well to consider the cooking technique as carefully as the ingredients.

Fresh—not smoked or cured—sausages also turn up in many English dishes. They are often pan-fried and served with mashed potatoes and caramelized onion gravy. The dish "toad in the hole" is a casserole of sausage links bathed in a light batter of eggs, flour, and milk, then baked. Interestingly, the name of the dish has been used in the United States to refer to a slice of toast with a fried egg cooked in a hole in the center. Street foods, the precursor to modern fast foods, also have roots in England with dishes like fried meat pies and fish and chips. In the case of fish and chips, the batter ingredients, dry and wet, must be combined and allowed to stand briefly before you dip the codfish fillets and fry them in hot oil. The end result is a tempura-like batter shell, rather than a breading in the traditional sense. The "chips" (think steak fries) are served with malt vinegar, which is milder and slightly sweeter than white vinegar.

Your ancestors with English roots may have recorded several curry recipes. During English colonial periods, those who spent time in India brought back an affinity for Indian spices. However, most "curry" recipes prepared by home cooks involve sprinkling a commercially prepared blend of curry spices onto a chicken or pot roast. Although traditional English teatime is no longer formally observed in most homes, you can see the legacy of the shortening-rich scones, sponge cakes, and cookies (biscuits) in the flaky biscuits, tea cakes, and chiffon cakes in many North American recipe boxes.

## France

French cooking often translates as "haute cuisine" to many Americans. And it's true that French cooks value high-quality ingredients and embrace the power of eggs, cream, and butter. However, there are regional variations in French cooking and plenty of everyday French dishes. *Cassoulet*—a humble white bean casserole made special with the addition of herbs, rich sausages, tender duck confit, and slow cooking—is quintessentially French. Ingredients are handled carefully, herbs infuse first the beans and then the final dish, and flavors are layered.

Depending on the area of France your ancestors called home, you might have family recipes that reflect the flavors of Provence—fresh vegetables, berries, tomatoes, olives, and a bold blend of aromatic herbs—or the region's famous *bouillabaisse* or the custom of serving thirteen desserts on Christmas Eve (to symbolize Christ and the disciples). You could have recipes that specify salt plain-raised sheep, or reflect the "marmite" fish stews, creamy sauces, and apple desserts found in Normandy. In some areas, the Algerian influence adds couscous, spicy harissa sauces, and dishes spiked with coriander and cumin. There are fondues throughout France, but especially in the French Alps; an abundance of sweet and savory crepe recipes from Brittany; and cabbage and sausage *choucroute* recipes of Alsace, to name a few traditions.

## Germany

Americans can thank German immigrants for the "All-American" hamburger, hot dog, and at least some versions of apple pie, not to mention bratwurst, potato salad, lager beer, and coffee cakes.

"Hearty" and "savory" are words frequently used to characterize German cuisine. The cold climate encourages a menu of calorie-dense foods, as well as ingredients that are cured, smoked, and pickled. Sausages star in many German dishes and may be grilled or boiled alone to serve as entrees. German cooks select from a list of some 300 *wursts* (German sausages) made from every edible part of locally raised pigs, beef cattle, and calves. *Braten* or roasts simmered in savory or sweet-and-sour sauces take center stage at many meals, often surrounded by baked or mashed potatoes, or potato pancakes. Red cabbage or turnips flavored with smoked meats, goose fat, vinegar, and sugar are served at meals with coarse, dark breads such as rye and pumpernickle. Strong flavors—onion, capers, mustard, horseradish, caraway seeds, and sour cream—figure into many dishes. Although some fish and poultry may be poached in wine, beer also is a favorite poaching medium.

North American families with German roots will likely have a rich repertoire of fruit-based desserts, such as apple dumplings, fruit pancakes, and jam-filled pastries to enjoy. Almond paste, rich Bavarian-style crème, and cream cheese–filled pastries are popular. For special occasions, elaborate creations such as Black Forest Cherry Cake appear. German culinary influences can be seen at US family tables in Pennsylvania Dutch country, in the upper Midwest, and in the barbecues of central Texas. German ingredients and cooking styles also overlap with many other Eastern European cuisines.

## Greece

Like cooks who prepare other Mediterranean cuisines, Greek cooks rely on olive oil, fresh fruits and vegetables, garbanzo beans, fresh fish and seafood (octopus and stuffed squid are favorites), and farmed whole grains. But if you're looking for elusive flavor, consider the cheese you're serving or adding to a recipe. In Greece, where feta cheese is a protected national product, the brined cheese comes in many different varieties—some soft, some crumbly, some mild, some tart, some slightly gamey, and some citrusy and sour. Authentic Greek

**FAST FACTS:** The delicate grace notes in extra-virgin olive oil disappear at high temperatures. That means you can use regular olive oil for cooking and save the expensive stuff for an accent at the end of cooking, for cold foods, and for lightly warmed dressings and sauces.

feta is always made from sheep's or goat's milk (usually sheep's), whereas similar types of cheese found in the United States and other areas may be made from cow's milk. Likewise, authentic Greek yogurt is a thick, tart staple and may be made from sheep's milk or cow's milk. Flavors vary depending on the type used. Yogurt can be seasoned for salads and savory dishes, or sweetened for use in desserts. Spinach figures prominently in Greek dishes, but Greeks also use a variety of other greens, including wild greens like dandelions. Greek olive oil and Greek oregano have distinctive flavor profiles. Greek halvah, unlike the crumbly sesame-paste candy served in other Mediterranean countries, is a gelatinous pudding made with semolina flour.

## Ireland

Although modern Ireland offers all the ethnic fare available throughout the Western world, the traditions likely carried to the United States and other locales by Irish grandmothers include many dishes born of subsistence farming and cooking. Irish soda bread—which is a crusty, round quick bread leavened with baking soda and buttermilk or sour milk instead of yeast—is a favorite dish. Some descendents add eggs, raisins, and other "sweet" items to the bread, but purists insist that it creates a different dish entirely. Cured meats and sausages, smoked and roasted salmon, root vegetables, mushrooms, and some dairy ingredients figure prominently, as does lamb and mutton. Coddle, a dish of layered sausage, sliced potatoes, bacon strips, and onions, and Irish stew, traditionally a slow-cooked pot of mutton, potatoes, onions, and other root vegetables, might be part of the family repertoire, although beef has replaced the mutton in many households. Old-line Irish cooks might remember stirring barley or oats into some stews to stretch ingredients. Unusual dishes like black pudding (a blood sausage made with congealed pig's or sheep's blood mixed with oatmeal or other grain) might be served at breakfast, which is usually a hearty affair with eggs, sausage, bacon, bread, and strong tea. Spices beyond salt and pepper are rarely used.

**FAST FACTS:** Refrigerated not-from-concentrate pineapple juice makes a great marinade for chicken. The enzymes in the juice help tenderize the chicken and, once the marinade is shaken off, the flavor isn't overpowering. Add garlic, spices, sesame oil, and soy sauce to the marinade for variety.

## Italy

It would take several volumes to cover the particular flavors, cooking techniques, and ingredients used in Italy, since Italian cooking actually comprises several regional culinary traditions. However, the traditions most frequently seen in North and South American households usually center on the cuisines of Campania and Sicily. Strong flavors dominate the cooking from Naples and the rural Campania area, with tomatoes, garlic, olives, artichokes, citrus fruits, anchovies, and peppers figuring prominently. Pasta is an essential, and it is combined with both cooked and barely cooked sauces of vegetables, fish, and some meats. Soft, water-buffalo-milk mozzarella cheese is a local staple, and the region can be thanked for classic thin-crust pizza and for layered "parmigiana" dishes, the original of which was made with thinly sliced, air-dried, lightly fried eggplant.

Sicilian cooking carries influences of all the conquerors and explorers that came through the island, particularly embracing the North African penchant for sugars and sweet dishes. Sicilian tomato sauces tend to be thicker and sweeter than other tomato sauce styles (and your Italian American grandmother probably calls them "red gravy"). Occasionally garden vegetables may be stewed together into something greater than the sum of their parts; for example, eggplant caponata. Fresh vegetables, lightly handled, figure prominently in Sicilian cuisine, and the volcanic soil of the island yields figs, grapes, pomegranates, melons, and dozens of different citrus fruits. If your recipes don't come out exactly like your great aunt Tina's, consider that she may have spent a great amount of time tracking down perfect, sun-ripened produce. Fresh tuna—pan-fried, grilled, or lightly sauced— is abundant in Sicily; however, Sicilian Americans may have switched to a tradition of canned tuna, which is often stirred into tomato sauce and served with spaghetti. Pine nuts appear in both sweet and savory dishes. Sicilian desserts like rich cassata cake, ricotta-filled cannoli, and beautiful marzipan fruits are the stars of celebrations and feasts, and families may have their own signature recipes, adjusting quantities of liqueur, flavorings, and other ingredients.

## Mexico

Most of the dishes identified as "Mexican" in the United States are either wholly American dishes or have been modified. Chili, for instance, has Mexican influences, but the dish was created in San Antonio. And few true Mexican taco recipes have big dollops of sour cream included in the ingredients.

Mexican cuisine is actually an age-old fusion of the diets of pre-Columbian indigenous peoples and Spanish settlers. If your family has Mexican or borderland roots, you'll find recipes where guava, papaya, avocado, tomatillos, peppers, and jicama figure prominently, as well as unusual seasonings like achiote, pumpkin seeds, and epazote. Corn is a staple for eating fresh, drying, and grinding into flour for tortillas and coatings, and for cultivating the beloved *huitlacoche* fungus—a mushroom-like growth that infects some corn ears. Cooks with Veracruz roots will likely have a bounty of seafood recipes, including a seafood-and-rice dish called *tumbada*. Many Veracruz recipes include a combination of tomatoes, olives, onions, garlic, and capers.

Vanilla, cinnamon, and chocolate turn up in pastries and other sweets. Chocolate is native, and unsweetened chocolate can be found in some savory recipes. It is the base for the Mexican national dish, turkey with mole sauce.

## Poland

Although North America has a large self-identified Polish population, there are many blurred edges because of the changing political borders and population shifts of Eastern Europe. That said, descendents of Poles can proudly claim a tradition of abundance and generosity where food is concerned, as well as some dishes that have translated to the modern world quite well. Pierogies, kielbasa sausages, and the almost elusively sweet babka cake can be found in many supermarkets, particularly in the Midwest. As with many Eastern European cuisines, one can find cooked and cured cabbage dishes, including sausage or pork roast and sauerkraut, fresh cabbage and noodles, and stuffed cabbage. Wild mushrooms figure prominently in Polish cuisine, as do organ meats and desserts of fried dough and even jam omelets.

## Writing Your Own Recipes

When putting together a keepsake cookbook, particularly a family cookbook, don't discount your own "oral tradition" recipes. When your children grow up, the unusual potato salad that you throw together with chilled, leftover baked potatoes, minced green onion, diced ham, and yogurt-laced mayonnaise is a dish they will crave. Likewise, your trick of using buttermilk instead of water in packaged muffin or cake mix recipes and your savory herb and cheese scones are part of the family repertoire. Your homemade white chocolate-cranberry-pecan granola bars? Priceless.

Give these dishes a name and write them down. Even if you usually work without instructions and add ingredients by feel, availability, or your own mood, take the time now to write what you do and give a guide for quantities ("⅓ to ½ cup chopped parsley or mixed fresh herbs" is fine). Your children and grandchildren will thank you!

## Managing Recipes from Several Contributors

Congratulations! You're putting together an extended family, neighborhood, or association cookbook and you've been tasked with coordinating the recipes. As head recipe wrangler, there are a few things you need to do or consider.

- Make a standardized label or short form or a digital header that will be attached to each recipe, whether the recipe is turned in as hard copy, on a flash drive, or as an e-mail attachment. You need to know who collected the recipe, their e-mail address or phone number, where they got the recipe, if they tested it, and the result. Also, any concerns about the recipe (difficulty, availability of ingredients, or other issues) should be noted. Make sure the recipe name, as noted on the recipe itself, appears on the label, just in case the label gets separated from the recipe (in the case of hard copy).

- Review this chapter with your contributors, explaining the nuances of collecting written recipes and coaxing not-yet-written recipes from friends and family members. If they're going to collect all the recipes they personally crave but don't have on hand, they'll need guidance.

- How many people will be contributing recipes? If the recipe committee consists of you and two to five other people and you expect dozens of contributors, it makes sense to divide the work according to types of dishes, branches of the family, or periods of history. Each committee member can compile a segment of the book. If the committee members *are* the contributors, then each person should prepare his or her own recipes, stories, pictures, and notes before turning the material over to the assigned copyeditor.

If you belong to a one-hundred-year-old quilting guild and you plan for your keepsake to illuminate the people and resources involved in each decade of the organization, you can assign two decades to each of five participants or committee members. Once the material has been amassed, the designated editor can sort the recipes into appetizers, soups, salads, and other categories, with eras and stories accompanying each recipe.

For three siblings putting together a family cookbook, each participant could take one or more cookbook categories and begin collecting recipes. Or each could research the recipes from a particular branch of the family.

If you belong to an organization with 200 members and you've launched your cookbook with an "open-door" policy, allowing everyone to contribute, then your editing role becomes extremely important. Make sure everyone understands the importance of attaching a label to each recipe and noting the contributor of the recipe as well the original source, if known. For instance, if you know that "Sandra's 1-2-3-4 Cake" originated on a box of Swan's Down Cake Flour, it's important to note that fact or mention that Sandra's version is an adaptation of the original.

**FAST FACTS:** Chinese wedding celebrations include a twelve-course banquet with all sorts of symbolic delicacies, including long noodles (for longevity) and a whole fish (for abundance).

Make digital or physical file folders for each contributor, each recipe category, each family branch, or each era before recipes start showing up on your kitchen table or in your e-mail directory. It doesn't matter how you divide the initial onslaught of recipes as long as you have a system that makes sense to you, and one that will allow someone else to assist you if needed.

After the recipes have been recorded and collected, you will be ready to move on to editing and, if needed, rewriting the recipes to get them into shape for your cookbook. We'll go over that process in the next chapter.

# Writing Recipes Like a Pro: Turning Grandma's Prose into Usable Instructions

You've collected a treasure trove of recipes. Your favorite cupcakes. Grandma's cranberry scones. Grandpa's stewed chicken and dumplings. Cousin Sarah's apple-walnut strudel. You may even have the collected recipes of your entire equestrian club or parenting pack. And now they're all sitting in a box, hard drive, or file folder. Some may still exist as e-mail attachments. Some are scribbled on the back of a shopping list, others are on coffee-stained and dog-eared index cards, and still others have been photocopied from a hand-written journal. What now?

Well, first you've got some organizing to do.

If your cookbook is built around a very narrow topic—say, Christmas cookies—you can simply flip through the recipes and decide on an appropriate order. Arrange them alphabetically if the collection is limited to a dozen or fewer recipes. For a larger collection, group the recipes by primary ingredient—for example, put the chocolate and chocolate chip cookies together, the fruit-filled cookies together, and the sugar cookies together. Or go with categories based on technique, grouping the drop cookies, the cut-out cookies, the bars, and the piped cookies in separate piles or folders.

A cookbook focusing on the broader category of desserts might have groups consisting of cookies and bars, cakes, pies and tarts, pastries, puddings and custards, mousses, soufflés, and frozen desserts.

For a general cookbook, go through the recipes and separate them into five folders: appetizers and hors d'oeuvres, soups, salads, entrees, and desserts. Later you can expand the entree category into distinct folders or digital subfolders for meats, chicken, fish and seafood, or any other grouping that makes sense given the number of recipes you have on hand. Desserts often break down into a cakes-and-pies category and another labeled "sweets" or "candies and confections."

In general, cookbook recipes should be divided using one of the following protocols:

- By course or food category

- By ingredient

- By menu

- By chronological era

- By geographic region or location

- By individual or family branch

- By occasion

When dividing recipes, you should attempt to have a similar number of recipes in each segment, rather than ten recipes for one decade and forty for the next. To achieve balance, you might want to reconsider your layout, or just insert subdivisions within some of the divisions. For example, a cookbook that's heavy on cookie recipes could have one section for drop cookies and another for bar cookies.

You can be creative in your segments, as long as the purpose is clear. In my memoir cookbook *Roux Memories*, I found creative category groupings that went well with the essays and photos I wanted to include. So in the book you'll find a chapter for boils, fries, and barbecues and another for pickles, preserves, and jellies. Those recipes might have fit in other categories as well, but I happened to like those groupings.

However you decide to divide the contributions, you or one of your collaborators will be rewriting or heavily editing most of the recipes.

## Writing Usable Recipes

Homegrown recipes rarely arrive "cookbook ready." Your mother's recipes may list ingredients according to quantity, importance, or expense. For example, Mom's Shrimp Stew could begin with "2 lbs cleaned shrimp" even though shrimp is the last ingredient added to the pot. Your grandpa's chili recipe might be written in prose, with quantities given in handfuls and pinches. That hundred-year-old custard tart recipe from your mother-in-law probably instructs cooks to bake the crust "blind." And your recipe box undoubtedly includes recipes with comments like "cook until done" or "makes a lot."

These recipes could be charming illustrations for your cookbook, especially if they're handwritten. Scan them and keep the originals for posterity. But they aren't in a form that will be helpful to future generations. Even recipes from professional chefs—often available for nonprofit fund-raiser cookbooks—are rarely written in standard household measurements since chefs generally work with ingredients by weight, not volume.

To make your cookbook a living treasure, this section will show how to write recipes in a standard cookbook format, with consistent terms, that can be used in the kitchen. Just follow these steps:

## 1. List ingredients in the order used to make the dish.

If you are making a stir-fry, you have a lot of trimming, dicing, and chopping to do before the meat and vegetables hit the wok. Unless you've got mad prep skills, it would be a mistake to start heating oil in the pan before the first head of baby bok choy has been rinsed. Instinctively, or through practice, you know this. But with some dishes, the order in which ingredients should be added may not be so obvious.

When a seasoned cook hands you a recipe that lists buttermilk, flour, eggs, butter, and sugar, followed by instructions that say "Mix well and bake in a medium oven," chances are that the cake won't turn out very well if the recipe is followed to the letter. Instead, you'll need to rewrite the ingredient list to be consistent with the most effective technique. The flour should be sifted together with any necessary salt or leavening agents, then set aside. Softened butter and sugar should be beaten until smooth and creamy. Eggs should be added to the butter mixture one at a time and beaten until the mixture is thick and light-colored. Then you should add some of the flour mixture, all the buttermilk, and then the rest of the flour mixture, followed by any extracts.

So the recipe for "Jo's Pound Cake" should begin with this ingredient list:

*Jo's Pound Cake*
  *3 cups flour*
  *2 teaspoons baking powder*
  *¼ teaspoon salt*
  *1 pound butter, softened*
  *2 cups sugar*
  *6 eggs*
  *1 cup buttermilk*
  *1 teaspoon vanilla or almond extract*

**FAST FACTS:** In New Orleans, where every holiday deserves a full slate of neighborhood parades, St. Patrick's Day "krewes" throw green beads and hand out cabbages to people along the parade routes.

Even if a recipe calls for an ingredient that will be added in two different steps, the ingredient is listed in order of first use. For example, let's say Jo's Pound Cake uses some "grated lemon zest" in the cake batter and some more sprinkled on a final glaze made from cream and confectioners' sugar. Three tablespoons will go into the batter and one tablespoon will be reserved for the glaze. The ingredients list would then look like this:

*Jo's Pound Cake*
   *3 cups flour*
   *2 teaspoons baking powder*
   *¼ teaspoon salt*
   *1 pound butter, softened*
   *2 cups sugar*
   *6 eggs*
   *4 tablespoons lemon zest, divided use*
   *1 cup buttermilk*
   *1 teaspoon vanilla or almond extract*
   *2 cups confectioners' sugar*
   *¼ cup heavy cream*

The expression "divided use" alerts the cook to the fact that an ingredient will be used in more than one step of the recipe. Divided use is often used in baked goods, where portions of flour are added at different stages, and in savory dishes, where chopped herbs or aromatic vegetables may be cooked into the dish and added at the end for garnish or texture.

Another way to handle ingredients used in multiple steps is to subdivide the recipe. This technique often appears in desserts or composed dishes that have clearly distinct stages. Once again, considering Jo's Pound Cake, the subdivided recipe ingredients would appear this way:

*Jo's Pound Cake*
   **Cake:**
   *3 cups flour*
   *2 teaspoons baking powder*
   *¼ teaspoon salt*

*1 pound butter, softened*
*2 cups sugar*
*6 eggs*
*3 tablespoons grated lemon zest*
*1 cup buttermilk*
*1 teaspoon vanilla or almond extract*

**Glaze:**
*2 cups confectioners' sugar*
*¼ cup heavy cream*
*1 tablespoon grated lemon zest*

**FAST FACTS:** Pennsylvania Dutch cooks have a tradition of including "seven sweets and seven sours" in family meals. Generally, the quantities are achieved by the use of pickles and relishes, which can be found in abundance in most households.

The decision to subdivide ingredients in a recipe is a personal choice, but when a dish has multiple stages, it definitely is the most reader-friendly option. Listing ingredients in the order of use, however, is not only the professionally accepted standard, it's the best way to avoid pound cake that begins as a flour-paste mess!

## 2. Don't use abbreviations.

Flip through the stack of homegrown recipes you've collected. You'll likely find an ingredient listing for a tablespoon measure of sugar expressed in each of these ways:

*1 T sugar*
*1 Tbsp sugar*
*1 TB sugar*
*1 heaping tablespoon sugar*

Maybe you know what the recipe author means, or maybe you can guess. But in a recipe where you've got tbsps and tsps, it's easy to wind up with a tablespoon of salt and a teaspoon of sugar instead of the other way around. Save yourself and your readers a lot of potential mistakes by writing out ingredients fully. So in a very simple recipe for meatballs, the ingredients list might look like this:

*1 pound ground beef*
*1 cup dried bread crumbs*

*1 egg*
*1 teaspoon salt*
*½ teaspoon black pepper*
*¼ teaspoon garlic powder*

Follow through with fully spelled-out measures in the recipe instructions and you'll help readers avoid mistakes.

### 3. Use common household measurements.

Pick up any cooking text written for professional chefs and you'll discover something interesting: Virtually all solid ingredient quantities are given by weight. A cup of flour will appear as 120 grams or 4½ ounces. Fluids will appear in volume measure, even if you're talking about eggs. There are good reasons for this—mostly having to do with the need for precision and uniform practice throughout the industry. (A pint of eggs could equal seven or eight eggs, depending on the size of the eggs you break.)

However, if you list a cup of flour as 4½ ounces in a cookbook aimed at home cooks, you're inviting disaster. Most home cooks will add a smidge more than half a cup to the recipe, reading "ounces" as an indication of volume rather than weight.

Food writers have guidebooks and pages of rules for writing recipe quantities, but for your purposes, try to think in terms of what makes sense and be consistent throughout your book. Here are some general rules:

Give quantities for raw meats, poultry, and seafood according to weight. Indicate whether the weight is for trimmed or untrimmed, bone-in or boneless, shelled or unshelled ingredients. For example:

*1 pound boneless pork loin, trimmed of fat*
*2 pounds large, head-on shrimp in the shell*
*1 pound lump crabmeat*

The exception to this rule is shelled raw oysters, which as a semisolid are generally packaged by volume weight (for instance, a pint of oysters).

Easily divided raw ingredients can be listed by count, or by a combination of count and weight. For example:

*1 dozen raw oysters on the half shell*
*4 boneless chicken breast halves*
*8 6-ounce filet mignons*

Solid or semifirm dairy products like chilled butter or cheese can be added to recipes by weight or volume, as long as the use is consistent throughout the recipe. Any cook should be able to determine what each of these quantities means:

*1 pound butter*
*1 cup butter, softened*
*½ cup melted margarine*
*1 pound cheddar cheese*
*2 cups shredded cheddar cheese*
*4 tablespoons crumbled Gorgonzola*

Cooked, prepared ingredients can appear by weight, piece, or volume, depending on the recipe. For example:

*2 cups diced roast chicken*
*1 pound cooked bulk turkey sausage*
*2 dozen broiled sea scallops*

Fruits and vegetables should be listed by piece or volume in most recipes. In some circumstances, where weights are easily discernible (for instance a three-pound bag of red potatoes), a weight measure can be given. However, most cooks cannot look at three medium tomatoes and know whether they have one pound or three pounds on the counter. Likewise, terms like *baskets* and *bushels* should be avoided in recipe lists. Here are few examples of proper quantity designations:

*1 medium zucchini*
*2 cups diced plum tomatoes*
*6 cups sliced peaches*
*1 5-pound bag white potatoes*
*6 large baking potatoes*

Liquids, of course, should be listed by volume, in tablespoons, ounces, cups, pints, quarts, and any fractions thereof. Use actual measuring tools, not "a tumbler full" or "a soup spoon." If you have to use a "can" as a measure (and there's no reason to pretend a can of condensed cream of mushroom soup is anything else), be certain to specify the size. For example:

*1 cup chicken broth*
*½ cup maple syrup*
*1 pint heavy cream*
*1 10-ounce can condensed cream of mushroom soup*

Finally, be sure to specify whether a measure should be taken before or after an ingredient has been cooked, drained, sifted, diced, or chopped. "One cup cooked, drained ground beef" is a greater amount of meat than either "1 cup raw ground beef" or "1 cup ground beef, cooked and drained." Sifted flour has been aerated, giving it greater volume and less density than unsifted flour. It may seem like a minor point, but readers and diners will appreciate the clarity.

## 4. Be clear about the best ingredients for your recipe.

Does it make any difference whether the pears in your dessert are firm or ripe? Should the ground beef in your chili be coarsely ground chuck or extra-lean ground round? Such distinctions affect not only taste, but texture and volume as well.

Be specific about varieties, size, ripeness, cuts, temperature, firmness, and any prep work, if such things are important to the dish. Small-diced plum tomatoes will give a different fresh salsa experience than peeled, coarsely chopped heirloom tomatoes. Would you rather have crisp bacon or soft-cooked bacon on your bacon and cheddar wrap? Will unpeeled potatoes change the color and mouth feel of your favorite chowder?

Don't make your readers guess which ingredients to select. Also, if there's an acceptable substitute for an ingredient in your recipe, make a note of it. Your caramel-drizzled poached pears may absolutely require fragrant, just-yielding Anjou pears. But if a time-pressed cook can substitute tart apples for the sliced pears in your pear-spice cake, be sure to let him or her know.

## 5. Write instructions clearly and logically.

Don't skimp on explanations. Your recipe instructions should begin with the first ingredient listed, then move step-by-step through each ingredient or group of ingredients. You should explain exactly what to do with each ingredient: how to handle it, how and when to add it, what follows the addition. The instructions for Jo's Pound Cake might begin like this:

1.  Preheat oven to 350°F. Sift flour, baking powder, and salt together into a medium bowl. Set aside.

2.  In a large mixing bowl, combine softened butter and sugar. Beat with an electric mixer on medium speed until mixture is smooth and creamy. Add eggs, one at a time, beating well after each addition. After the last egg has been added, beat the mixture on medium-high speed until light-colored and fluffy, about 4 minutes.

Even an inexperienced cook can look at the ingredients, look at the instructions, and know that the flour, baking powder, and salt must be sifted, the moist ingredients must be combined in a particular way, and the mixing should continue for several minutes.

It's hard to overestimate the importance of good instructions—particularly when translating heirloom recipes for a modern audience. Imagine a recipe for cream puffs that begins with an ingredient list of butter, water, flour, and eggs, followed by instructions that say "Make choux pastry." Maybe a few cooks will know to boil the butter and water, stir the flour into the boiling mixture, continue stirring until a smooth dough forms, then cool the mixture before beating in the eggs, one at a time. Most will not. They'll either have to research the method or just give up. Likewise, a cake recipe that essentially says "mix everything and bake until done" isn't helpful.

Some recipe writers like to number the steps in their instructions, while others just make a new paragraph for each step. Such niceties are strictly a matter of personal preference. The important thing is to make sure all variables have been covered. Here's a checklist to help:

- Are all items in the ingredient list addressed individually in the instructions? Do they appear in the instructions in the same order as they appear in the ingredient list?

- Do the instructions specify how an ingredient should be added to the recipe? Should it be stirred by hand, mixed with an electric mixer, gently folded in with a spatula, sifted, carefully added to a hot mixture, tempered with a small amount of hot liquid, or added all at once or a little at a time? If you simply say "Add parsley," it must be acceptable to throw all the parsley into the mix without further attention.

- Have you specified what kind of vessel should be used? A glass baking dish will give a different texture to baked goods than an aluminum or cast iron pan. What size pot or pan? Does the shape matter and should it have a lid?

- How should the cooking pot or pan be prepared? Should it be greased, and if so, with what? Is a parchment paper liner required? Should the wok or skillet be preheated? Do the jars need to be sterilized?

- Does the oven, grill, or stove need to be preheated? If so, to what temperature?

- Have you told the reader how long the dish should cook, at what temperature, and whether any adjustments should be made while the food is cooking?

- Do the instructions tell the cook how and when the dish can be served? Meats, casseroles, and most baked goods need to rest for a few minutes before being cut or removed from the pan.

## 6. Don't forget to include the recipe yield.

You can express the quantity produced by a recipe in number of servings, volume, or pieces, depending on the recipe. Baked goods usually are expressed as number of pieces, such as "Makes 1 9-inch Bundt cake" or "Makes 3 dozen gingersnaps." Entrée recipes usually specify the number of people served, as in "Makes 6–8 servings." Some condiments and sauces can be expressed as volume measures, such as "Makes 4 pints jam."

Remember to give realistic yields or specify volume. A serving of mashed potatoes, according to the US Department of Agriculture, is one-half cup. That said, a cook who makes four cups of mashed potatoes and expects to serve eight people is doomed to be embarrassed. A more accurate yield would be "Makes 4–6 servings."

**FAST FACTS:** The Memphis in May festival includes the week-long World Championship Barbecue Cooking Contest. Internationally renowned as the Super Bowl of Swine, the contestants cook nearly 19,000 pounds of barbecue.

## Giving Proper Credit

Numerous legal eagles, including the US Copyright Office, have concluded that a list of ingredients, however unique or interesting, cannot be copyrighted. However, a "substantial literary expression" such as a description or illustration, or a collection of recipes, may be eligible for a copyright. That means recipe instructions, recipe notes, and ingredient glossaries may or may not be protected. Food essays, remembrances, and entire cookbooks are more likely to be protected.

In reality, most standard recipes can't be copyrighted because only original material can be protected. Your garden-variety cake, roast chicken, grilled cheese sandwich, and tossed salad—even with that great white balsamic vinaigrette—aren't going to qualify as original material.

That said, there is honor among food writers. If the family from-scratch chocolate cake recipe comes from the back of a cake flour box, say so. If you use the recipe as a base from which to experiment with mocha, chocolate-toffee, and white chocolate flavors, note that your recipe was "adapted from" the XYZ Company recipe. Likewise, if your favorite casserole began as a soup-company recipe, give a nod to the source.

At the very least, in your cookbook you should credit the person from whom you got the recipe or the one who is most closely associated with the dish. If your keepsake cookbook is a group project, credit the recipe contributor and any person he or she wishes to acknowledge.

In my memoir cookbook *Roux Memories,* I have recipes credited to aunts and uncles who are very unlikely to have invented the dishes that bear their names. However, my Aunt Lillian—a good Cajun cook—is the first person who served me chicken cacciatore. So I built the recipe in the book around my memory of that childhood meal and gave her credit. You'll find Nan Rita's Benne Pralines and

## Format for Recipes

**Title** Can be bold, upper- and lowercase in larger type, or all capital letters.

**Ingredients** Must be listed in order of use in the recipe.

**Instructions** Should be broken into manageable steps, with no more than two or three sentences per step. Steps can be separated as paragraphs or numbered.

**Yield** How many servings does this recipe make? Can be listed as a range.

**Source** If known and not a family member referenced in the title or text.

**Note** Optional. Only if needed.

**Details:**
- All references should be consistent. If you refer to "granulated flour" in one recipe and "sauce and gravy flour" in another, it will be confusing. Butter can be ¼ pound or a stick, but it shouldn't be both.
- Measurements should be for ingredients as they will be added to the recipe. In other words, "1 cup parsley, chopped" means a cup of parsley leaves that will then be chopped, resulting in about ½ or ⅔ cup parsley. If you want a full cup of chopped parsley, say so.

Audrey's Seafood Gumbo in the book, both of which came to me in written recipes from the authors.

However, many recipes in the book are uncredited because they were originated, first written, or perfected by me, or because they're part of the general Cajun-Creole repertoire of dishes. I can tell you how my family prepared crawfish etouffee, but I certainly can't tell you that anyone in my family invented the dish, nor do I have any idea who did. The word *etouffee* means "smothered" in French, and that generally translates to something prepared via a braising technique. So I know the dish has French roots and so do most of my relatives. Is it my recipe? Absolutely. I've made it for family and friends since I was sixteen years old. Have I adapted it to my own taste preferences? Sure. Is it original? Probably not.

- Measurements should not be abbreviated. Teaspoon, tablespoon, cup, quart, and so on should be written out.

- Terms like "medium oven" are confusing to most young cooks. Say 350°F. Low, medium, and high can be used for stovetop cooking, where dials usually specify those settings.

- Yield is a subjective thing. Generally speaking, a home-style entree serving of soup, stew, chili, or gumbo will be a 12-ounce bowl, which means a 2-quart batch will serve 6. An appetizer portion is 8 ounces. Quantity/serving guidelines are available online; however, you should use your best judgment on servings based on your family eating habits.

- Sources: Give credit if the source of the recipe is known. You should write the instructions, in a consistent manner.

- Recipe notes: A recipe note can be an ingredient explanation, a technique explanation, or an author's tip. ("Make the dish, except for the added sour cream, a day ahead of time for best flavor.") It also can explain things like "Grandma made this dish with lard, but vegetable oil or half oil/half butter will work just fine."

In a keepsake cookbook, the route a recipe took to find its way to your table and to your cookbook is sometimes as interesting as the recipe itself. The more people you can include in your food memories, the more compelling the story will be. So it's in your interest to be generous with credit.

To be on the up-and-up, follow these guidelines:

- Write from scratch any recipe you personally add to the cookbook.

- Credit anyone who gave you a recipe or influenced one.

- Ask contributors where they got a recipe. If the recipe came from an identifiable source, mention it.

- To call an adapted recipe your own, the rule of thumb is to make three substantial changes to the ingredients or preparation method.

- Recipes on state and federal government websites and in government publications are available for anyone to use. Feel free to use them, but do note the source.

- Likewise, many trade organization and food company recipes are up for grabs. Look for an indication that the recipes can be used, or ask permission. Either way, give credit.

- If you aren't sure of the source of a recipe, say so. In my cookbook I have a family-favorite dessert that looks like it probably came from an old cake mix recipe brochure. I can't find the original recipe, but I do note that it looks suspiciously like a corporate recipe.

## Testing Recipes

Testing each and every recipe in your cookbook is a great idea—and if you have the time, inclination, and resources, by all means do so. If you plan to sell your book, you owe it to purchasers to know that each recipe works. That said, if you have a stack of written recipes from family and friends—recipes that they use regularly—you probably don't need to test every single one of those dishes. Your contributors, in effect, have tested those recipes for you. In fact, if you're editing recipes from the cookbook committee for a group or organization, you should insist that they come to you already tested.

That said, you should test any recipe that you build from an oral discussion about a dish, any recipe that comes to you written very generally, any recipe you re-create from memory, and any recipe that just doesn't look right.

Recipes should be tested from your final version. Follow the steps exactly as you have them written, not from memory, and not as you think the recipe should have been written. Only after testing the recipe you plan to give to others as finished instructions can you ensure that they will get the proper result. Once you've tested a recipe and decided it needs tweaking, make the adjustments, rewrite the recipe, and test it again.

If you have friends or family members who volunteer to help test recipes and you trust their basic cooking skills, by all means take them up on the offer.

## Deciphering Heirloom and Ethnic Recipes

If you're lucky, you'll have many generations-old recipes to include in your cookbook. And you'll have to translate vintage expressions and unusual ingredients, measures, and technique names into readable ingredients and prose. Following are some of the terms you may encounter and what they mean.

*Alligator pear*  A term still used in some circles. Refers to an avocado.

*Baking powder biscuits*  Baking powder biscuits are the biscuits most of us prepare and eat. The term "baking powder" added to the name is merely a way to distinguish the biscuits from English crackers and cookies, and from yeast-raised biscuits.

*Blind*  To bake a crust "blind" means to put it in the oven without a filling or topping. In modern recipes, this is just expressed as partially baking the crust or spreading the crust in the pie pan and baking at a given temperature for a given length of time. Blind baking would be used for a crust that will be filled with an unbaked filling, or a crust that should be partially baked before filling to keep it from getting soggy.

*Bread starter*  This technique is still used by sourdough bread fans. It refers to a mixture of flour and water, or sometimes a bit of dough from a previous bread batch, that is allowed to ferment and attract wild airborne yeasts. The starter is then used to leaven homemade bread.

*Buttercream*  In modern home recipes, buttercream frosting is the name given to an uncooked mixture of butter, confectioners' sugar, and flavoring—maybe with a splash of cream thrown in. Vintage recipes are more likely to be referring to the French-style buttercream, made with beaten eggs or egg yolks.

*Calf's head hash*  Shockingly to modern sensibilities, this is exactly what it sounds like. A calf's head is boiled, and the meat is removed and added to a sauce of flour, butter, seasonings, and broth. The brains are usually cooked separately and served on a platter with the hash.

*Castor sugar*  Another name for superfine sugar that dissolves quickly.

*Certified milk* Before most commercially available milk was both pasteurized and homogenized, there were dairies and farms that sold unpasteurized or "raw" milk that was determined by local inspectors to have been produced in sanitary conditions. Substitute ordinary whole milk.

*Chess pie* A popular southern US dessert made from eggs, sugar, butter, and flavoring. The pie filling bakes into a rich custard. Some food etymologists believe the name of the dish is a corruption of "cheese," with initial devotees mistaking it for (or serving it in place of) a cheesecake of some variety.

*Chinese rice* No, this isn't jasmine, basmati, or sticky rice. In vintage cookbooks, Chinese rice refers to the way most cooks steam rice today: by combining 1 cup rice with 1½ cups water and cooking over low heat, covered, for 20 minutes.

*Dragées* In vintage recipes, this term could be used for hard, candy-coated almonds (aka Jordan almonds), or it could refer to the little, hard, silver-colored sugar balls used to decorate wedding cakes and holiday cookies. Those metallic dragées are considered to be inedible by the US government, although they are sold for decorative purposes in most states. And, truth to tell, anyone who's ever been to a communion, wedding, or Christmas cookie swap has probably eaten a few.

*Earthen pan* A term for ceramic or crockery cookware that may or may not be glazed. In many instances, a glass baking dish or casserole can be substituted.

*English peas* Synonymous with green peas.

*Frizzle* Recently, some restaurant menus have included "frizzled" spinach, which is deep-fried spinach leaves. In older recipes, the term usually refers to pan-frying thin-sliced meats, like ham, until the edges become curled and crispy.

*Gill* A gill is a liquid measure that's equivalent to half a cup.

*Gratons* Used in French-derived recipes to refer to pork cracklings, which are diced, deep-fried bits of pork belly.

*Gruel* No, this isn't a workhouse joke. Gruel is a boiled mixture of oatmeal or cracker crumbs, usually strained and laced with milk. It was considered good for restoring health and strength to ailing persons.

*Haggis* This Scottish favorite, lauded by poet Robert Burns, is an acquired taste. The heart, lungs, and kidneys of a sheep are minced and mixed with oatmeal, onion, broth, and spices. Then this organ meat loaf mixture is sewn into the cleaned stomach of a sheep and simmered for several hours. The cooked haggis is cut and eaten with root vegetables. Modern versions are sometimes stuffed into a large sausage casing instead of a stomach.

**FAST FACTS:** Floridians argue that the first Thanksgiving meal on American shores occurred in St. Augustine, Florida, more than fifty years before the Pilgrims' feast. Spanish explorer Pedro Menéndez de Avilés landed on the site of America's oldest city in September 1565. He and his shipmates celebrated a Mass and a meal of thanksgiving with the Timucua Indians that likely included beans, olive oil, pork, biscuits, jam, wine, and, from the Timucuans, oysters and giant clams from the nearby waters.

*Head cheese* You can buy this stuff in meat markets and supermarkets today. But your grandparents probably made their own. Head cheese is made by boiling the scrubbed and trimmed head of a freshly slaughtered pig. Tender bits of meat from the long-cooked skull (and possibly some boiled vegetables) get chopped and placed in a pan or mold. The cooking liquid is strained over the chopped bits and refrigerated. The liquid sets into a firm aspic, suspending the meat and vegetable bits. Head cheese is served cold and sliced with crackers or bread.

*Italian rice* This term sometimes is used when referring to arborio or risotto rice.

*Mexican sauce* No, not enchilada sauce, tomatillo sauce, or even queso. In very old recipes, Mexican sauce is likely to refer to a white sauce that has been rendered pink through the addition of strained pimentos and studded with diced bell peppers.

*Paris sticks* Another name for almond meringue cookies, piped in lines onto cooking parchment.

*Pearlash* This appears only in very old cookbooks and recipes. Pearlash is made from wood ashes and is a substance once used to leaven dough. It has been replaced in the modern kitchen with baking powder.

*Peck* A quantity of produce equivalent to two gallons.

*Periwinkles* Periwinkles, also known as winkles, crinkles, and winks, are small sea snails collected from the rocky shores of the northern Atlantic and a few other areas around the globe. They can be eaten raw or cooked.

*Pickled fruits* Peaches, plums, pears, cherries, and crabapples were often pickled in a sweet-tart brine by nineteenth- and early-twentieth-century cooks. Thus preserved, the fruits were then served as condiments beside savory dishes.

*Perloo or pilau* A corruption of the word *pilaf,* referring to a mixture of rice, fish or fowl, plus seasonings and pan drippings. Whereas a pilaf tends to be a side dish, Southern pilaus are meatier and serve as main dishes.

*Potted meats* Early-twentieth-century cooks "potted" everything from calves' tongues to liver to veal shanks. The term refers to browning and braising meats with aromatic vegetables in a covered vessel. The term "pot roast" is probably derived from this.

*Rich milk* Independent dairies often produced and sold milk with a higher percentage of butterfat than can be found in whole milk today. Use half-and-half or a mixture of whole milk and half-and-half to re-create a recipe calling for rich milk.

*Ris de veau* French term for calf sweetbreads. Sweetbreads are the thymus gland of a young animal.

*Rivels* A mixture of flour and egg or flour and water that can be either pinched or drizzled into boiling water or soup to create small, free-form noodles. The process of pinching the dough is sometimes referenced as riveling.

*Saratoga chips* A mid-nineteenth-century creation of a chef in Saratoga, New York. You probably know them better as potato chips and probably get them premade from a bag. However, if you can learn to make ultra-thin-sliced, flash-fried homemade chips, you'll never want the commercial stuff again. Try serving them hot with a crumble of Gorgonzola cheese.

*Satsuma soup* A Japanese-inspired soup that has nothing to do with the satsuma citrus fruit. The dish is a mélange of chicken, miso, tofu, and greens that appeared on North American menus in the early 1900s.

*Scald* To cook a liquid, usually milk, to a temperature of 196°F, which is 18 degrees lower than boiling.

*Sour milk* Buttermilk, or whole milk that has been curdled by the addition of a small amount of vinegar or lemon juice. Does not ever refer to milk that has gone bad in the refrigerator.

*Spring chicken* A young, not fully matured chicken, which would be more tender than a fully grown hen. A hundred years ago, these birds would weigh about 1½ pounds. However, today we would use fryers, which are now bred to weigh twice as much. The cook might need to adjust quantities for other ingredients in the recipe accordingly.

*Syllabub* Although it sounds like the name of some sort of Goethe-esque creature, this term refers to an alcoholic milk punch, generally made from some combination of brandy, white wine, sugar, lemon, and cream. Beaten egg whites might be added to give the mixture "froth."

*Sugar cream pie* A dessert usually credited to the Amish of Indiana. Although it appears similar to Southern "chess" pie, an authentic sugar cream pie contains sugar, butter, and cream, but no eggs.

*Sweet butter* Butter that is unsalted.

*Sweet milk* This isn't condensed milk. It's a reference to ordinary whole milk, as opposed to buttermilk. Your updated recipe should read "milk."

*Thanksgiving pudding* A somewhat odd concoction that's a cross between custard and bread pudding. It's a traditional egg-milk-sugar custard that's laced with raisins and nutmeg and thickened with cracker meal. As with ordinary custards, this one bakes for more than two hours at low heat.

**FAST FACTS:** For years, France and Italy laid claim to the best truffle-hunting grounds in the world. However, the state of Oregon is quickly catching up. Since 2005, the Oregon Truffle Festival near Eugene has attracted truffle hunters, chefs, and diners from all over the world. One of the most popular events? The session where you can learn to train your own dog to be a truffle-hunting dog.

*Tortes* Often used in modern cookbooks to refer to any sort of layered dessert or savory appetizer. In vintage cookbooks, entire chapters exist for *torten*, which refers to butterless cakes made from whipped egg whites, ground nuts, sugar, sometimes bread or cracker crumbs, and flavorings. The layers bake in springform pans and may be filled with different fruit or custard fillings.

*Venison jelly* No, not another form of head cheese. Venison jelly is a clove-and-cinnamon-laced jelly made with Concord grapes and vinegar. This condiment was considered a good complement to venison roasts, hence the name.

**5**

# Basic Cookery: Tips, Timing, and Techniques

Maybe you're a great cook. Maybe you've put together a whole keepsake cookbook committee full of great cooks. But at some point in the cookbook-writing process, you're going to thank me for this chapter. Because at some point, you're going to be writing, editing, or testing a recipe in the collection and you're going to say, "Uh . . . that doesn't look right." And you're going to want a quick-and-easy way to double-check cooking times, ingredient amounts, and techniques.

In this chapter you'll find safety tips, cooking time charts, and food terms, as well as some very basic home-cooking recipes. That way, if Aunt Dina's 3-pound beef-and-pork meat loaf recipe says it cooks in 30 minutes and serves 4, you will have a point of reference for changing that information (long before anybody gets sick from eating raw ground pork).

And here's a bonus: You also can use the information and charts in this chapter to add content to your own cookbook. The material either comes from my own experience as a food writer, or, in the case of the food safety guidelines and safe cooking times, it comes from the US Department of Agriculture and other US government agencies.

## Food Safety

My grandmother kept baskets of eggs on the kitchen table and my mom used to thaw meat on the counter. I have old cookbooks that instruct cooks to let cooked strawberry jam sit in a pot overnight before ladling it into jars.

Fortunately, no one in the family got sick from these unsafe practices, but I'd never tempt fate that way today.

Here are a few general safety rules, followed by some food-specific guidelines.

- Keep it clean! Wash kitchen surfaces with antibacterial wipes, soaps, or cleaners; wash dishes and utensils in hot, soapy water; and wipe cooktops and oven handles frequently.

- Keep cold foods cold and hot foods hot. Never allow cooked or perishable foods to sit at room temperature for more than two hours. Bacteria grows in the temperate zone between 40°F and 140°F.

- Avoid cross-contamination. Store raw meats, poultry, and fish separately and keep all raw proteins away from cooked foods, fruits, and vegetables.

- Marinades used to flavor and tenderize raw meats, poultry, and fish should not be reused as is. If you're willing to drain the marinade into a pan and bring it to a full boil on the stove, you can use it as a basting agent during cooking.

- Never put cooked meats, poultry, or fish on a platter where raw ingredients have been . . . unless, of course, you wash the platter in warm soapy water in between.

- Don't defrost food on the kitchen counter. Yes, that includes the Thanksgiving turkey. Allow enough time for foods to defrost in the refrigerator. Or defrost in a pan of cold water, changing the water completely every 30 minutes.

- Meats defrosted in a microwave must be cooked immediately after defrosting because some parts of the meat may have begun to cook.

- Never partially cook or brown meats or poultry and then return the ingredients to the refrigerator. Complete the cooking process, cool, then chill. Don't put piping-hot food directly into the refrigerator. This can cause uneven chilling, which encourages the growth of bacteria.

- Check your refrigerator and freezer temperatures periodically. The refrigerator should be no higher than 40°F and the freezer should be 0°F.

- Wash your hands. Before and after handling food, lather up with antibacterial soap.

## Poultry

- Raw poultry may contain any of several bacteria associated with food-borne illness. These bacteria are killed by thoroughly cooking the poultry to an internal temperature of 165°F.

- Whole chickens, turkeys, and other fowl should be stuffed immediately before roasting. Prestuffing the bird can cause bacteria to multiply in the stuffing.

- Raw thawed poultry can be stored in a refrigerator for one to two days before cooking.

- Cooked poultry, including fast-food and take-out chicken, should be refrigerated promptly and eaten within three to four days.

- Frozen chicken that has been wrapped and has not been allowed to thaw at any point can be cooked and eaten within a year.

- Frozen chicken can go directly into the oven or into a pot on the stove. It cannot be safely cooked in a microwave or slow cooker without being thawed.

## Beef

- Raw beef may contain any of several bacteria associated with food-borne illness. These bacteria are killed by thoroughly cooking meats to an internal temperature of 145°F for steaks and roasts, 160°F for ground and chopped meats.

- Raw beef steaks and roasts should be kept refrigerated and cooked within three days; raw organ meats and ground meats, within one to two days.

- Well-wrapped beef can be frozen for nine to twelve months without loss of quality.

- All rare-cooked meats have the possibility of being contaminated with bacteria. However, the risk is even greater with rare ground meats.

## Pork and Ham

- Trichinosis is the most widely known risk factor associated with eating undercooked pork. Although the incidence of the parasite in fresh pork has been reduced, it remains a threat, as do several other illness-causing bacteria. Cooking pork to an internal temperature of 160°F kills all these microorganisms.

- Refrigerate raw pork in a pan with sides or in a resealable plastic bag. Use or freeze raw pork within two to three days. Ground pork is highly perishable and should be cooked within one day.

- Leftover cooked pork should be eaten within three to four days.

- Frozen pork cuts should be eaten within four to six months and frozen dishes made with pork should be thawed and eaten in two to three months.

- Use refrigerated, cured, but uncooked ham within five to seven days, or if vacuum-sealed, by the "use-by" date. Eat cooked leftovers within three to five days.

- Ready-to-eat, vacuum-sealed ham will keep in the refrigerator for two weeks or until the "use-by" date. Conventionally wrapped and spiral-cut hams will keep three to five days.

- Frozen cooked ham should be eaten within one to two months.

- Fresh, uncooked ham should be cooked to an internal temperature of 160°F, and uncooked cured ham to a temperature of 160°F. Cooked and vacuum-sealed ham can be heated to 140°F and repackaged cooked ham to a temperature of 165°F.

- Cured country ham may have harmless mold on the rind. Simply rinse the ham and scrub off the mold with a vegetable brush before cooking.

- Soaking country ham in several changes of cold water can help reduce saltiness.

## Fish and Shellfish

- Use fish and seafood within two days of purchase. Keep refrigerated and well-wrapped.

- Frozen seafood should be eaten within three to six months.

- Oysters are filter feeders. That means they may harbor pathogens from the waters in which they live. Raw oysters carry a risk of *Vibrio vulnificus* bacteria in particular, which can be deadly to people with compromised immune systems.

- Pregnant women, the elderly, children, and people who have compromised immune systems should not eat raw or undercooked shellfish and fish, nor refrigerated cured or smoked fish that is uncooked.

- Pregnant or nursing women should not eat fish with high levels of methylmercury, including swordfish, shark, tilefish, and king mackerel. Albacore tuna and tuna steaks have elevated mercury levels as well.

- Crabmeat must be fully cooked. Most peeled crabmeat available in fish markets and grocery stores is pasteurized, frozen, or canned. Raw crabmeat is translucent; cooked is opaque.

- Raw fish can contain worms and other parasites. If you plan to enjoy sushi made with raw fish, freeze the fish first to kill any worms and reduce the risks.

- Buy fish from reputable sources and know where the fish or seafood came from. Fish and seafood are only as "clean" as the waters in which they live and breed.

## Eggs

- Raw eggs carry a risk of *Salmonella* bacteria. The risk in fresh, properly stored shell eggs is relatively small, but the results of salmonella poisoning can be devastating. In recipes that will remain uncooked, consider using pasteurized shell eggs.

- Never feed raw or undercooked eggs to small children, the elderly, or people with autoimmune disorders.

- Throw away any eggs that are cracked in the carton.

- Keep eggs in the carton in the coldest part of the refrigerator.

- Use eggs within a month of the sell-by date on the carton.

- Unpeeled boiled eggs will remain edible for one week if stored in the refrigerator.

## Cooking Times

These cooking times reflect the best cooking times for a list of common dishes and ingredients. This isn't a food safety list, because a pot roast will likely be safe to eat long before it's tender and delicious. (Actually, time isn't the best indicator of food safety. The best indicator is internal temperature.) Use an instant-read thermometer to ensure that your meats, poultry, and seafood reach the following temperatures:

Beef and Bison Roasts, Steaks – 145°F
Chicken Breasts – 165°F
Eggs – 160°F
Fish – 145°F
Ground Beef – 160°F
Pork – 160°F
Whole Poultry – 165°F

| Meat | Weight | Temperature | Minutes Per Pound |
|---|---|---|---|
| Beef tenderloin | 6 pounds | 425°F | 12 |
| Beef rib roast | 6 to 8 pounds | 325°F | 27 to 30 |
| Veal loin roast | 3 pounds | 325°F | 20 |
| Leg of lamb | 9 pounds, bone-in | 325°F | 30 |
| Pork ribs | 4-pound rack | 325°F | 30 |
| Pork tenderloin | 1 pound, boneless | 425°F | 28 |
| Pork crown roast | 10 pounds | 325°F | 20 |
| Ham, ready to cook | 8 pounds | 325°F | 20 |
| Whole turkey, unstuffed | 12 pounds | 325°F | 15 |
| Whole chicken, unstuffed | 5 pounds | 325°F | 20 |
| Salmon fillet | 1 pound | 350°F | 15 |

## A Guide to Less-Than-Exact Quantities

When deciphering great-grandma's recipes (or even your mother's), you're likely to need a translation for some of the measures used.

*Measures*

Pinch = ⅛ teaspoon

Smidge = ½ teaspoon

Handful = ¼ cup

Ladleful = ½ cup

"Glass" or tumbler = 1 cup

Juice glass = 4 ounces

Soup spoonful = scant tablespoon

Cooking spoonful = ¼ cup

Jigger = 1½ liquid ounces

Half an eggshell = about 2 tablespoons or 1 ounce volume

Slow oven = 300°F.

Moderate oven = 350°F

Good-sized = generally recognized as being slightly larger than the average size for the ingredient in question

*Weight conversions*
>  One pound flour = 4 cups
>  One pound sugar = 2¼ cups
>  One pound brown sugar, packed = 2⅓ cups
>  One pound confectioners' sugar = 4 cups
>  One pound shelled eggs = 10 large eggs

*Volume conversions*
>  1 cup = 16 tablespoons
>  1 stick butter = 8 tablespoons or ½ cup
>  4 sticks butter = 1 pound
>  4 tablespoons = ¼ cup
>  1 tablespoon = 3 teaspoons

## Basic Recipes

Use these standard recipes as a guide for timing and technique when making other versions of the same dishes. Your chicken soup, cranberry sauce, or meatballs may have different seasonings or a different sauce, but the method of preparation, cooking time, and servings will be similar.

### Mixed Green Salad

>  *6 cups assorted salad greens, rinsed and dried*
>  *1 cup shredded red cabbage*
>  *½ cup sliced radishes*
>  *½ cup sliced celery*
>  *½ cup sliced carrots*
>  *½ cup diced bell pepper*
>  *1½ cups grape tomatoes or 1 cup diced tomato*
>  *1 cup trimmed, diced cucumber*
>  *⅔ cup fresh berries, diced apple, diced pear, or dried cranberries*
>  *1 cup prepared vinaigrette-type salad dressing*
>  *1 cup crumbled or shredded cheese of your choice*
>  *2 cups croutons or 1 cup toasted nuts*

1. In a large salad bowl, combine greens, cabbage, radishes, celery, carrots, and bell pepper. Toss to mix ingredients.

2. Shortly before serving, toss in tomatoes, cucumber, and fruit.

3. Shake or whisk the salad dressing until well blended. Pour half the dressing over the salad and toss to coat ingredients with dressing. Add more dressing as desired.

4. Sprinkle cheese and croutons or nuts over the top of the salad.

MAKES 8 SERVINGS.

*Note:* Add 3–4 cups of diced chicken or turkey, boiled shrimp, or steak to make a main-dish salad.

## Balsamic Vinaigrette Dressing

*⅔ cup extra-virgin olive oil*
*⅓ cup vegetable oil*
*½ cup balsamic vinegar*
*1 teaspoon Dijon mustard*
*1 garlic clove, pressed*

Combine all ingredients in a deep bowl. Whisk together until dressing is thick and all ingredients have been well blended. Use immediately or transfer the dressing to a covered jar or cruet.

MAKES 1½ CUPS DRESSING.

## Fresh Tomato Salsa

*5 ripe medium tomatoes, small diced*
*1 small onion, finely chopped*
*1–2 jalapeño peppers, minced*
*⅓ cup cilantro, finely chopped*
*2 cloves garlic, minced*
*2 tablespoons parsley, finely chopped*
*2 tablespoons lime juice*

1. Combine tomato, onion, and jalapeño peppers in a large bowl. Toss well. Fold in cilantro, garlic, parsley, and lime juice.

2. Cover and refrigerate at least 1 hour before serving.

MAKES 3 CUPS SALSA.

## Whole Cranberry Sauce

*1 cup sugar*
*½ cup orange juice*
*½ cup water*
*12 ounces fresh cranberries*
*2 tablespoons orange zest*

In a medium saucepan, bring sugar, juice, and water to a boil. Add cranberries and orange zest. Let mixture come to a boil again, reduce heat, and simmer 10 minutes until berries burst. Cool, then cover and store in the refrigerator until ready to use.

MAKES 2½ CUPS.

## Senate White Bean Soup

*2 pounds dried navy beans*
*1½ pounds smoked ham hocks*
*1 onion, chopped*
*2 tablespoons butter*
*Salt and pepper to taste*

1. Wash navy beans in a colander. Pick out any dark beans, small pebbles, or specks of dirt.

2. Place beans in a heavy soup pot with 4 quarts of water. Add ham hocks and bring mixture to a boil over high heat. Reduce heat to medium, cover pot, and cook, stirring occasionally, for 3 hours.

3. Remove the ham hocks from the soup and set aside to cool. Cut meat from the ham hocks, dice or shred, and return to the soup pot.

4. In a skillet over high heat, sauté onion in butter until lightly browned. Pour contents of skillet into the soup. Season with salt and pepper.

MAKES 8 SERVINGS.

## Old-Fashioned Chicken Noodle Soup

**Stock:**

*1 stewing hen, about 5–6 pounds*
*1 onion, quartered*
*1 small bunch parsley, rinsed*
*1 green onion, halved*
*3 ribs celery, cut in thirds*
*3 carrots, cut in thirds*

**Soup:**

*1 rib celery, thinly sliced*
*1 carrot, thinly sliced*
*1 cup peas*
*1 cup dry medium-width noodles*
*¼ cup minced parsley*
*Salt and pepper to taste*

**Make stock:**

1. Rinse hen and remove giblets. Reserve giblets for another use.

2. Place hen in a large, heavy soup pot with enough cold water to cover. Add onion, parsley, green onion, celery cut in thirds, and carrot cut in thirds. Bring water to a boil over high heat, then reduce heat to medium-low. Simmer for 2 hours. Remove from heat and let cool until chicken can be handled safely.

3. Remove chicken from the broth. Remove meat from the chicken, cover, and refrigerate.

4. Return chicken carcass and skin to the broth. Cook over medium-low heat for 6 to 8 hours. Remove from heat. Strain the broth through a fine

sieve into a clean soup pot. There should be 10 cups. If less than 10 cups, add more water.

**Make soup:**

1. Let broth stand briefly and skim off any fat that rises to the top. Add sliced celery and sliced carrot. Stir in peas.

2. Cook over medium heat for 5 minutes. Raise heat to high and bring broth to a boil. Add noodles, stirring to disperse. Cook, stirring frequently, until noodles are tender, about 8 to 10 minutes.

3. Reduce heat to medium-low. Chop or shred reserved chicken meat. Add to the broth and simmer 5 minutes. Add parsley. Season with salt and pepper to taste and serve.

MAKES 8 SERVINGS.

## Simple Chili with Beans

*2 pounds lean ground beef*
*1 medium onion, diced*
*1 medium bell pepper, diced*
*4 tablespoons chili powder*
*½ teaspoon cumin*
*1 14-ounce can pinto beans, black beans, or kidney beans*
*2 15-ounce cans tomato sauce*
*1 10-ounce can tomatoes and green chiles*
*3–4 cups water or beef broth*
*Salt and pepper to taste*

1. In a large, heavy saucepan, combine ground beef, onion, and bell pepper. Cook over medium-high heat, stirring to break up the beef.

2. When ground beef is completely browned, drain off fat. Sprinkle meat mixture with chili powder and cumin. Stir well.

3. Add beans, tomato sauce, tomatoes and green chiles, and 3–4 cups water

or broth to the pot. Cook over medium heat for 1 hour, stirring often. Add water as needed.

4. When chili reaches desired thickness, season with salt and pepper. Remove from heat. Let cool slightly and serve.

MAKES 8 SERVINGS.

## Pot Roast

⅓ cup granulated flour
1½ teaspoons salt
1 teaspoon black pepper
¼ teaspoon cayenne pepper
¼ teaspoon garlic powder
1 4-pound rump roast or boneless chuck roast
¼ cup olive or vegetable oil
1 large onion, diced
1 rib celery, sliced
2 cloves garlic, minced
1 tablespoon ketchup
2 cups beef broth
1 bay leaf
½ cup red wine, optional
1 tablespoon cornstarch
3 tablespoons cold water

1. Combine granulated flour, salt, black and cayenne peppers, and garlic powder. Sprinkle seasoned flour over the roast, rubbing to coat all sides.

2. Heat a heavy Dutch oven over high heat. Add oil. Brown roast on all sides, turning carefully.

3. Add onion, celery, and garlic to the pot. Stir, scraping the pot as you do, for 2 minutes. Stir in ketchup and beef broth. Add bay leaf and reduce heat to medium-low. Cover the pot and cook for 2 hours, stirring and turning the beef occasionally.

4. Remove beef to a platter. Over high heat, bring pan drippings to a boil. Add wine, if desired, and cook 3 minutes.

5. Dissolve cornstarch in cold water, stirring well to remove any lumps. Add cornstarch mixture to the pan, stirring to blend. Cook until gravy is thickened and translucent. Remove from heat. Strain into a gravy boat or over sliced roast.

MAKES 6–8 SERVINGS.

**FAST FACTS:** There are several types of corkscrews available to home cooks, but the best choice is the lever or rabbit-style corkscrew. This type of corkscrew works in a continuous motion without the need for extra muscle. Lever corkscrews are more expensive than ordinary models but are less likely to leave you with cork in your wine bottle or wine splashed on your counter. The second best (and considerably cheaper) choice is a winged corkscrew. The pocketknife-looking version that waiters carry is only an option if it's well made and you're willing to spend a lot of time practicing.

## Meatballs

*1 pound ground beef*
*1 pound ground pork or veal*
*2 tablespoons ice water*
*2 eggs*
*1½ cups soft bread crumbs*
*2 tablespoons minced parsley*
*Salt and black pepper to taste*
*Cayenne pepper to taste*
*1 cup granulated flour*

1. Preheat oven to 325°F.

2. In a large bowl, combine beef and pork or veal. Place the meat in a food processor. Working in batches and adding a few drops of ice water to each batch, pulse the meat a few times.

3. Return the finely ground beef and pork or veal to a bowl. Combine with eggs, bread crumbs, and parsley. Add salt, pepper, and cayenne to taste.

4. Work ingredients with hands until very well blended. Roll meat mixture into 24 meatballs. Roll meatballs lightly in flour and place, not touching, in a baking pan.

5. Bake at 325°F for 15 to 20 minutes, turning occasionally to brown on all sides.

6.  Remove from oven. Add to sauce of choice or cool completely, place in resealable plastic bags, and refrigerate or freeze for later use.

MAKES 24 MEATBALLS.

*Note:* For cocktail meatballs, roll mixture into 36 meatballs and cook 10 to 12 minutes.

## Meat Loaf

*2 pounds ground beef, or a combination of ground beef and ground pork*

*2 eggs*

*1½ cups bread crumbs or 1 cup rolled oats*

*1 cup milk or tomato sauce*

*⅔ cup finely chopped onion*

*⅓ cup diced bell pepper*

*1 clove garlic, pressed*

*¼ teaspoon Worcestershire sauce*

*¼ teaspoon cayenne pepper*

*Salt and pepper to taste*

*⅓ cup ketchup*

1.  Preheat oven to 350°F.

2.  In a large bowl, combine ground meat with eggs and mix with hands until well blended. Add bread crumbs or oats, along with milk or tomato sauce. Mix well. Work in onion, bell pepper, garlic, Worcestershire sauce, cayenne, and salt and pepper. Mixture should be thick and hold together easily. (If mixture seems too soft, add more bread crumbs.)

3.  Shape the mixture into a firm, oval-shaped loaf. Place the loaf in a baking dish and bake for 45 minutes.

4.  Carefully spoon the ketchup over the center of the loaf and continue baking for 15 minutes. Remove from oven and let stand 10 minutes before slicing.

MAKES 8 SERVINGS.

## Roasted Chicken

1 5–6-pound roasting chicken
2 tablespoons olive oil
3 cloves garlic
1 medium onion, peeled and halved
1 lemon, quartered
1 teaspoon kosher salt
½ teaspoon black pepper
¼ teaspoon cayenne pepper
1 teaspoon fresh rosemary leaves

1. Preheat oven to 350°F.

2. Rinse chicken and remove giblets. Reserve giblets for another use. Pat chicken dry and place in a shallow roasting pan. Coat chicken with olive oil. Press garlic and rub garlic pulp over the chicken.

3. Place onion and lemon in the chicken cavity. Combine kosher salt, black pepper, and cayenne pepper. Sprinkle over the top of the chicken, followed by the rosemary leaves.

4. Bake chicken for 1 hour 40 minutes, or about 20 minutes per pound. Remove from the oven. Let rest 20 minutes before carving.

MAKES 6 SERVINGS.

## Rosemary-Garlic Tenderloin of Beef

4 pounds beef tenderloin
1 tablespoon olive oil
3 cloves garlic, pressed
½ teaspoon freshly cracked black peppercorns
1 tablespoon fresh rosemary leaves
Salt to taste

1. Preheat oven to 450°F.

2. Place tenderloin in a roasting pan and coat well with olive oil. Spread pressed garlic evenly over the roast and sprinkle with black pepper and rosemary.

3. Reduce heat to 350°F. Roast tenderloin, uncovered, 1 hour for medium to medium-rare. Sprinkle with salt in the last few minutes of roasting. Let stand for 10 to 15 minutes before slicing.

MAKES 8 SERVINGS.

## Fried Pork Chops

8 boneless pork loin chops, about ¾-inch thick
2 eggs
½ cup milk
2 teaspoons salt
1 teaspoon black pepper
1 teaspoon cayenne pepper
½ teaspoon paprika
1 teaspoon garlic powder
1½ cups flour
½ cup panko-style bread crumbs or regular dry bread crumbs
2–3 cups vegetable oil

1. With a sharp knife, trim pork chops of excess fat. Set aside.

2. In a wide bowl, whisk together eggs and milk.

3. In a cup, combine salt, black pepper, cayenne pepper, paprika, and garlic powder. Stir with a fork or small whisk. Sprinkle half the seasoning mix into the eggs and milk.

4. On a plate or in a pie pan, combine flour, bread crumbs, and the remaining seasoning blend. Stir with a dry fork to mix well.

5. Dip four of the pork chops in the egg mixture, allowing excess to drip back into the bowl, then dredge in the flour mixture.

6.  Pour oil in a deep skillet or Dutch oven to a depth of 2 inches. Heat over high heat until oil reaches 350°F.

7.  Carefully slide the four battered pork chops into the oil. Cook 4 minutes, then turn with tongs. Continue cooking 5 minutes. Remove chops to a platter lined with paper towels.

8.  While the first four chops are cooking, dip the remaining chops in the egg mixture and dredge in the flour mixture. Add to the hot oil after cooking the first batch of chops. Cook 9 to 10 minutes, turning once. Drain on paper towels.

MAKES 8 SERVINGS.

## Chicken Fajitas

**Fajitas:**

*8 boneless chicken breast halves*
*½ cup lime juice*
*1 cup olive oil, divided use*
*4 garlic cloves, pressed*
*2 teaspoons salt*
*½ teaspoon black pepper*
*¼ teaspoon chipotle pepper*
*1 teaspoon cumin*
*½ teaspoon dried oregano*
*2 bell peppers, preferably different colors*
*2 large onions*
*16 flour tortillas*
*1 pound shredded cheddar or Mexican blend cheese*

**Condiments:**

*Salsa*
*Sour cream*
*Guacamole*

1. Place chicken breasts in a resealable plastic bag. Combine ½ cup lime juice, ½ cup of the olive oil, and pressed garlic. Pour into bag over chicken, seal, and place bag in a baking dish in the refrigerator for 4 hours or overnight. Turn bag occasionally.

2. Remove chicken from marinade, shaking off excess liquid. Discard marinade.

3. Combine salt, black pepper, chipotle pepper, cumin, and oregano. Sprinkle seasoning mix over chicken breasts.

4. Trim bell peppers and onions and cut into strips lengthwise.

5. Place a large, heavy skillet over high heat. When the skillet is just hot, pour some of the remaining olive oil in the skillet, add chicken breasts, and sear for 2 minutes on each side. Reduce heat and continue cooking until chicken breasts are no longer pink (about 5 to 7 minutes, depending on thickness).

6. Remove chicken to a platter. Slice across the grain into thin strips.

7. Turn up heat on skillet and stir-fry peppers and onions over high heat for 2 minutes.

8. Spoon over chicken strips and serve with warm tortillas and shredded cheese. Pass condiments as desired.

MAKES 8 SERVINGS.

## Shrimp Creole

⅓ cup melted bacon grease
1 large onion, diced, divided use
1 small bell pepper, cored and diced
1 rib celery, chopped
3 garlic cloves, minced
3 large fresh tomatoes, peeled, seeded, and chopped
1 teaspoon sugar
¼ teaspoon cayenne pepper

*2 cups shrimp or chicken broth*
*1 15-ounce can tomato sauce*
*1 teaspoon Tabasco sauce*
*2 pounds medium shrimp, peeled*
*¼ cup minced fresh green onion*
*¼ cup minced fresh parsley*
*Salt and black pepper to taste*
*6-8 cups steamed rice*

1.  In a Dutch oven over high heat, combine bacon grease and half the onions. Cook, stirring constantly, until onions begin to brown, about 10 minutes.

2.  Add remaining onion, bell pepper, celery, garlic, and tomatoes to the Dutch oven. Reduce heat to medium and cook, stirring often, until vegetables are crisp-tender and tomatoes begin to release juice.

3.  Add sugar, cayenne pepper, and 1 cup broth. Simmer for 10 minutes, then add remaining broth, tomato sauce, and Tabasco. Simmer mixture for 20 minutes, stirring often.

4.  Add raw shrimp to sauce and cook just until shrimp turn pink. Stir in green onion, parsley, and salt and black pepper to taste. Serve over steamed rice.

MAKES 6 SERVINGS.

## Poached Salmon
*⅔ cup white wine*
*⅔ cup water*
*1 tablespoon orange juice*
*1 stick cinnamon, optional*
*1 onion, sliced*
*2 sprigs fresh dill*
*2 slices lemon*
*4 salmon fillets, about ½ pound each*
*Salt and pepper to taste*

**FAST FACTS:** Be careful when adding alcohol to dishes you plan to serve to children or teetotalers. The "bite" from wine and other spirits burns off after 30 seconds in a simmering broth or sauce. However, some alcohol remains in the dish. It takes more than an hour of cooking to remove most of the traces of alcohol.

1.  Combine wine, water, and orange juice in a large skillet over high heat. Add cinnamon stick if desired. Arrange onion slices, dill, and lemon in the liquid. Bring liquid to a boil, then reduce heat to medium. Simmer for 3 minutes.

2.  Sprinkle salmon with salt and pepper. Add salmon fillets to the liquid, skin side down. Cover skillet and poach fillets for 10 minutes.

3.  Remove salmon to a platter. Serve with Cucumber-Dill Sauce.

MAKES 4 SERVINGS.


## Cucumber-Dill Sauce

*1 cup sour cream*
*2 tablespoons mayonnaise*
*1 teaspoon prepared horseradish or Dijon mustard*
*¼ cup minced fresh dill*
*½ cup grated, seedless cucumber*
*⅛ teaspoon curry powder or cumin (optional)*

1.  In a small bowl, combine sour cream, mayonnaise, horseradish or mustard, and dill.

2.  Whisk until blended.

3.  Place the grated cucumber in a sieve and press as much of the water out of the cucumber as possible. Stir in cucumber and curry powder or cumin. Cover and refrigerate until ready to use.

MAKES 1¾ CUPS.


## Mashed Potatoes

*1 5-pound bag russet potatoes*
*¼ pound butter*
*¾ cup hot milk*
*Salt and pepper to taste*

1. Rinse potatoes to remove loose dirt. Peel potatoes. Cut each in half lengthwise, then crosswise into uniform, thick slices.

2. Place potato pieces in a large soup pot or Dutch oven with enough cold water to cover. Bring to a boil over medium-high heat. Boil potatoes, adding more water if needed, until a fork inserted in a slice penetrates easily—about 20 minutes.

3. Carefully remove pot from heat and drain potatoes in a colander. Add butter to the now-empty cooking pot. In a microwave or on the stove, heat the milk until just hot, not boiling. Remove pot from burner. Return the well-drained potatoes to the pot, along with half the milk.

4. Using an electric mixer on low speed, begin breaking up the potatoes. As the lumps disappear, increase speed to medium and whip until smooth, adding more milk as needed for desired consistency.

5. Add salt and pepper to taste, mix well, and serve.

MAKES 8 SERVINGS.

## *Steamed Long Grain White or Jasmine Rice*

*1 cup long grain white or jasmine rice*
*1½ cups water*

1. Measure rice into a fine sieve and rinse. Combine rice and water in a saucepan with a tight-fitting lid. Bring to a boil over high heat.

2. Cover the pot and reduce heat to medium-low. Cook 20 minutes. Remove from heat, fluff, and serve.

MAKES APPROXIMATELY 3 CUPS COOKED RICE.

## *Sautéed Broccoli*

*1 head broccoli*
*1 tablespoon olive oil*
*1 tablespoon butter*

*1 garlic clove, slivered*
*Salt and pepper to taste*

1.  Rinse broccoli and cut off 2–3 inches of the woody stalk. Cut the head in half lengthwise.

2.  Bring a large kettle of water to a full rolling boil. Drop broccoli into the water and blanch for 2 minutes. Remove halves from the boiling water and rinse with cool water. When broccoli can be handled, cut into florets or spears.

3.  In a wok or sauté pan, combine olive oil, butter, and garlic over high heat. Cook for 30 seconds, then add broccoli pieces. Continue cooking on high heat, stirring often, for 3 to 5 minutes. Add salt and pepper to taste.

MAKES 4–6 SERVINGS.

## Banana Cream Pie

*⅓ cup cornstarch*
*2 cups half-and-half*
*¾ cup sugar*
*3 egg yolks, beaten*
*1 tablespoon butter*
*1 teaspoon vanilla*
*3 small bananas, sliced*
*1 9-inch vanilla wafer piecrust*
*3 cups whipped cream*

1.  Dissolve cornstarch in 1 cup cold half-and-half. In a deep saucepan, heat remaining half-and-half over medium heat. Whisk in sugar and egg yolks. Bring mixture to a boil, then add half-and-half with cornstarch.

2.  Reduce heat to medium-low and cook, stirring constantly, for 10 minutes or until mixture thickens. Remove from heat and stir in butter and vanilla. Cool to room temperature.

3. Distribute half the banana slices over the bottom of a vanilla wafer piecrust. Spoon a layer of custard mixture over the bananas. Top the custard with remaining bananas and remaining custard.

4. Cover and refrigerate until well chilled. Before serving, top with whipped cream.

MAKES 6–8 SERVINGS.

*Note:* To make coconut cream pie, just add 1 cup shredded coconut to the custard while still warm, and sprinkle ½ cup toasted coconut over the whipped cream. Omit the bananas.

## Key Lime Pie

**Crust:**
*16 graham crackers, finely crushed*
*¼ cup sugar*
*1 stick butter or margarine*

**Filling:**
*4 large egg yolks*
*1 14-ounce can sweetened condensed milk*
*½ cup Key lime juice, freshly squeezed*
*2 teaspoons grated Key lime zest*
*Whipped cream (optional)*

**Make crust:**

Combine cracker crumbs and sugar. Melt butter or margarine and mix ingredients thoroughly. Press into a glass or ceramic 9-inch pie pan and bake at 350°F for 10 minutes. Set aside to cool.

**Make filling:**

1. In a large bowl, beat the egg yolks until light and slightly thickened. Add sweetened condensed milk. With an electric mixer on low speed, beat in half the lime juice, mixing until well blended. Add the remaining lime juice and zest and mix until thoroughly incorporated.

2. Pour mixture into pie shell and bake at 350°F for 12 minutes. Remove from heat and cool completely, then refrigerate for several hours. Serve with whipped cream if desired.

MAKES 8 SERVINGS.

*Note:* Before we all knew about salmonella in eggs, most cooks would not have baked the filling. The acid in the lime juice thickens the eggs and condensed milk without heat. Baking the pie does give it a slight custard flavor, but it also kills parasites and ensures you won't be making anyone ill. As an alternative, you can use pasteurized shell eggs and skip the baking step.

## Chocolate Cake

*2 cups cake flour*
*2 cups sugar*
*⅛ teaspoon salt*
*½ teaspoon baking powder*
*½ cup butter*
*2 eggs*
*¾ cup buttermilk*
*¾ cup water*
*1 teaspoon vanilla*
*4 ounces unsweetened chocolate, melted*
*3 cups Chocolate Buttercream Frosting*
*2 cups chopped praline pecans*
*1 cup white or dark chocolate curls for garnish*

1. In a large bowl, combine flour, sugar, salt, and baking powder.

2. In another large bowl, combine butter and eggs; beat on medium speed until mixture is light and creamy.

3. Sift dry mixture into the butter and eggs. Beat with an electric mixer on low speed to combine, adding buttermilk in a slow stream. Add water and vanilla. Beat on medium speed for 1 minute. Add melted chocolate and beat an additional minute.

4.  Pour batter into two greased 9-inch cake pans. Bake at 350°F for 25 minutes or until a toothpick at the center of the layers comes out clean. Cool in pans for 10 minutes, then turn layers onto racks and cool completely.

5.  Place one layer on a cake plate. Spread chocolate buttercream frosting over the layer. Place remaining layer over the filling and frost the outside of the cake with buttercream. Gently press chopped praline pecans into the sides of the cake and garnish the top with chocolate curls.

MAKES 1 9-INCH CAKE.

## Chocolate Buttercream Frosting

1 cup butter, softened
4–5 tablespoons heavy cream
1 tablespoon espresso or strong coffee
5 tablespoons regular or dark cocoa
6 cups confectioners' sugar
1 teaspoon vanilla

1.  In a large bowl, combine butter and heavy cream. Beat with an electric mixer on medium speed until light and creamy. Beat in espresso or strong coffee.

2.  In another large bowl, combine cocoa and confectioners' sugar. Whisk to aerate and remove any lumps.

3.  Add dry mixture to butter, a little at a time, beating on medium-low to incorporate sugar. If, after adding all the sugar, the mixture seems stiff, add another tablespoon of cream. Finally, beat in the vanilla extract.

FILLS AND FROSTS A 2-LAYER CAKE.

## Buttermilk Chocolate Chip Pound Cake

3⅓ cups all-purpose flour, divided use
2 teaspoons baking powder
½ teaspoon salt

*1 pound butter, softened*
*3 cups sugar*
*6 eggs*
*1¼ cups buttermilk*
*1 teaspoon vanilla*
*1 12-ounce package mini chocolate chips, divided use*
*1½ cups confectioners' sugar*
*⅓ cup heavy cream*

1. Preheat oven to 350°F.

2. Spoon out ⅓ cup flour and set aside. Sift remaining flour, baking powder, and salt into a small bowl.

3. In a large bowl, combine butter and sugar. Beat with an electric mixer on low speed until mixture is creamy and well blended. Add eggs one at a time, beating well after each addition. Change mixer to medium speed and beat 2 minutes, until batter is thick and light in color.

4. Combine buttermilk and vanilla. Add ⅓ of the flour mixture to the egg batter and mix well. Add half the buttermilk and continue mixing, followed by another third of the flour, the remaining buttermilk, and the remaining flour. Beat at medium-high speed until batter is smooth, about 1 minute.

5. Remove 2 tablespoons chocolate chips from the package; set aside. Toss remaining chips with the reserved ⅓ cup flour to coat. Carefully stir the chips into the batter with a wooden spoon or spatula.

6. Pour the mixture into a greased and floured 10-inch Bundt or tube pan. Bake at 350°F for 60 to 80 minutes or until a tester inserted in the cake comes out clean. Allow cake to cool 10 minutes before turning onto a cake plate. Allow cake to cool completely.

7. Whisk together confectioners' sugar and cream to make a smooth glaze. Drizzle the glaze over the top of the cake, then sprinkle reserved chocolate chips over the glaze.

MAKES 12 SERVINGS.

## Blueberry Crumb Muffins

**Batter:**

1½ cups flour

1 cup sugar

½ teaspoon salt

1 tablespoon baking powder

½ cup melted butter

2 eggs

⅔ cup milk

1 teaspoon vanilla

1½ cups blueberries

**Topping:**

⅓ cup flour

¼ cup chilled butter

⅓ cup brown sugar

1 teaspoon cinnamon

**FAST FACTS:** The groom's cake is a tradition that originated in the southern United States, where the traditional frilly white wedding cake became known as the bride's cake. Early groom's cakes were similar to modern rum cakes and bourbon-soaked fruitcakes, while the modern version is more likely to be chocolate.

**Make batter:**

1. Preheat oven to 375°F.

2. In a large bowl, combine flour, sugar, salt, and baking powder. Stir with a whisk to remove any lumps. Reserve 2 tablespoons of dry mixture.

3. Whisk together butter, eggs, milk, and vanilla. Add to dry mixture and whisk until just blended and no large dry lumps remain. Toss blueberries with reserved flour mixture. Fold berries into batter.

4. Pour batter into 12 large, greased muffin cups.

**Make topping:**

1. In a small bowl, combine flour, butter, sugar, and cinnamon. Cut together with two knives or a pastry blender until mixture resembles coarse crumbs. Sprinkle topping over muffin batter.

2.  Bake at 375°F for 20 to 25 minutes. Serve warm with butter.

MAKES 12 MUFFINS.


## Nestle Toll House Cookies

2¼ cups all-purpose flour
1 teaspoon baking soda
1 teaspoon salt
1 cup (2 sticks) butter, softened
¾ cup white sugar
¾ cup packed brown sugar
1 teaspoon vanilla extract
2 large eggs
2 cups or 1 12-ounce package semisweet chocolate chips
1 cup chopped nuts

1.  Preheat oven to 375°F.

2.  Combine flour, baking soda, and salt in a small bowl.

3.  Place butter, white sugar, brown sugar, and vanilla extract in large bowl. Beat with an electric mixer on medium speed until creamy. Add eggs, one at a time, beating well after each addition. Gradually beat in flour mixture. Stir in morsels and nuts.

4.  Drop by rounded tablespoons onto ungreased baking sheets.

5.  Bake for 9 to 11 minutes or until golden brown. Cool on baking sheets for 2 minutes; remove to wire rack to cool completely.

MAKES ABOUT 48 COOKIES.

*Source:* Nestle Toll House Test Kitchen

## Sugar Cookies

1 pound butter
1 cup white sugar
½ cup brown sugar
1 egg
3 tablespoons evaporated milk
2 teaspoons vanilla or almond extract
3 cups flour
1½ teaspoons baking powder
½ teaspoon salt
Large-crystal colored sugar or sprinkles

1. Place butter in a large bowl at room temperature. Allow to reach very soft consistency.

2. Add white and brown sugars to the butter. Beat with an electric mixer at medium speed until mixture is creamy and well blended. Beat in egg, milk, and extract.

3. In another bowl, combine flour, baking powder, and salt. Whisk to aerate and break up any lumps.

4. Add flour to creamed mixture in batches, beating until each addition is well blended.

5. Cover bowl and refrigerate until dough is chilled, about 15 minutes.

6. Preheat oven to 350°F.

7. Drop cookies onto an ungreased baking sheet by the rounded teaspoonful. Sprinkle with sugar or sprinkles, if desired.

8. Bake for 6 to 8 minutes or until cookies are very lightly browned. Cool in pan for a few minutes, then carefully transfer to cooling racks. Cool completely, then store in a tightly covered container.

MAKES ABOUT 48 COOKIES.

## Do-It-Yourself Pizza

Maybe your heirloom recipes include pizza, and maybe they don't. The one thing we know is that everybody loves pizza of some kind. Today supermarkets carry decent ready-to-top crust, as well as fresh pizza dough to allow cooks to make "from scratch" pizza. And some cooks make pizza crust the old-fashioned way, with or without an assist from a bread machine.

The following lists give the basic amounts of ingredients needed to top a 12-inch pizza, plus a full spectrum of ingredients to inspire you or your readers. Use the lists to create your own pizza recipes for your cookbook, or give your readers the lists, adding any ingredients you wish.

### ¾ CUP SAUCE

Pizza sauce
Thick pasta sauce
Alfredo sauce
Chunky salsa
Barbecue sauce
Teriyaki sauce
Pesto sauce
Peanut sauce
Queso sauce
Cranberry sauce
Refried beans

### 2 CUPS CUBED OR SHREDDED CHEESE

| | |
|---|---|
| Mozzarella | Edam |
| Provolone | Gruyére |
| Parmesan | Emmenthaler |
| Romano | Manchego |
| Asiago | Feta |
| Cheddar | Queso blanco |
| Colby | Brie |
| Brick | Camembert |
| Monterey Jack | Port salut |
| Gouda | |

# Basic Cookery

**Here's how it works:**

1. Choose one item, or a blend of items, from each list.

2. Preheat oven to 400°F.

3. Put the ingredients, in the amounts specified at the top of each list, on a 12-inch pizza crust of your preferred variety. Add minced fresh garlic or fresh herbs if you like.

4. Place on a perforated or deep-dish pizza pan or pizza stone. Bake at 400°F until browned and bubbly. Let stand briefly, then slice and serve.

MAKES 4 SERVINGS

## 1 CUP PRIMARY TOPPING

Sliced or diced pepperoni
Shredded beef
Ground beef
Sliced meatballs
Bulk sausage
Sliced sausage
Diced ham
Sliced Canadian bacon
Shredded pork
Shredded chicken
Fried chicken nuggets
Fried catfish nuggets
Diced boiled or roasted
  chicken
Diced grilled chicken
Ground turkey
Chopped turkey
Sliced duck
Chopped veggie burgers

Chopped veggie
  sausage
Chopped broccoli
Chopped cauliflower
Chopped spinach
Diced artichokes
Sliced eggplant
Diced zucchini
Diced yellow squash
Sliced mushrooms
Blanched asparagus
Diced fresh tomatoes
Chopped or whole
  shrimp
Chopped lobster
Diced scallops
Lump crabmeat
Sliced fresh tuna
Flaked salmon

## ½ CUP ACCENT TOPPING

Diced onions
Sliced green onions
Diced or stripped bell peppers
Chopped hot peppers
Sliced green or black olives
Capers
Crumbled bacon
Diced tasso
Sliced fennel
Chopped water chestnuts
Diced bamboo shoots
Smoked fish
Toasted nuts
Pumpkin seeds
Raisins
Dried cranberries
Diced apples
Diced pears
Crumbled blue cheese
Crumbled Gorgonzola cheese
Diced tofu

93

## Cooking Terms

Here are a few definitions to help you understand the recipes you collect, and, if you're the group cookbook editor, know what your recipes are asking cooks to use or to do!

*A la mode* Typically on American menus and recipes, *a la mode* means something served with ice cream or frozen yogurt on top, as in Apple Pie a la Mode. However, the term actually refers to any presentation that involves a topping.

*Al dente* Literally means "to the teeth." Used to refer to the stage of cooking when the pasta is tender but firm.

*Arborio* Thick, short grain rice used to make risotto. Similar in density to Valencia rice, which is used in paella.

*Arrowroot* A starchy white powder used in place of cornstarch or flour as a thickener in some recipes. Derived from the roots of the arrowroot plant.

*Bain-marie* A pot or pan of water into which another pan—holding the ingredients to be cooked—is placed. This coddling protects delicate mixtures from direct heat.

*Beurre manié* Equal amounts of butter and flour, worked together to form a soft, cold paste. (Think of it as raw roux.) Small lumps of *beurre manié* can be added to sauces to thicken and enrich the mixture.

*Blanch* To cook or partially cook vegetables and other ingredients by briefly plunging them into boiling water, then removing them to a bowl of ice or cold water to stop the cooking process. Vegetables can be blanched in boiling water for a few seconds or up to 2 minutes.

*Bouquet garni* A small bundle of aromatic herbs either tied together or placed in a cheesecloth pouch. The usual ingredients include bay leaves, thyme sprigs, and parsley sprigs.

*Braise* To brown ingredients at high heat, then simmer in a small amount of liquid over medium heat until tender.

*Brine* A seasoned saltwater or water-and-acid mixture used to flavor and tenderize poultry, particularly turkey.

*Brown* To cook meats, vegetables, and other ingredients over high heat long enough to turn the surface area a rich brown color. Browning caramelizes the natural sugars present in food, adding another dimension of taste, texture, and color to recipes.

*Buckle* A fruity coffee cake made by pouring a simple sweet batter over a pan full of berries or sliced fruit. Buckles usually have some type of crumb or streusel topping.

*Caramelize* To cook something until the natural sugars in the meat, vegetable, fruit, or dairy product begin to turn into a golden, syrupy liquid.

*Chiffonade* A big word for a simple step. Herbs or leafy greens sliced horizontally into thin strips, often used in salads and as garnish.

*Chili vs. Chile* *Chili* is the universally accepted spelling for a stew made from meats or beans, seasoned with mild to hot peppers. *Chile* is the spelling some writers and growers use to distinguish the peppers from the dish. However, you will also see the term "chili peppers" used.

*Chili powder* Commonly used to refer to a spice blend that includes capsaicin powder (red pepper), cumin, garlic powder, oregano, and possibly other ingredients. Different blends have different dominant flavors, and some cooks prefer to make their own.

*Clarified butter* Ordinary butter contains milk solids that can burn at high temperatures. Clarifying removes these solids. Gently melt butter over low heat, then pour into a clear measure or gravy separator. The solids will settle to the bottom. Siphon off the clear liquid to another container. Use as directed.

*Coddle* To cook slowly in a container placed in or above gently simmering water. Often used for eggs and delicate custards.

*Coulis* A strained fruit or vegetable puree that can be used as a smooth sauce.

*Cream* To beat together a solid fat and sugar until the mixture takes on a light and fluffy texture and the sugar is completely dispersed in the butter or shortening. Used as a noun, of course, it refers to the butterfat-rich liquid skimmed from the top of undiluted milk.

*Curry* In the United States and other Western countries, *curry* usually refers to a ubiquitous spice blend called *curry powder*. A dish seasoned with this mix is considered "curried." However, in Asian countries, *curry* refers to both seasoning blends and to a dish itself. Indian curries may contain turmeric, cumin, cinnamon, cloves, cardamom, fenugreek, and red pepper. Thai curries are more likely to feature lemongrass, kaffir lime leaves, galangal root, tamarind paste, hot chiles, and coconut milk.

*Divided use* An indication that an ingredient will be used in two places in the recipe and the amount given covers both additions.

*Fold* To gently incorporate an aerated ingredient—usually egg whites or whipped cream—into a thicker liquid or batter. Cooks use a circular or folding motion to turn the batter onto itself, carefully mixing in some of the egg whites or cream with each turn.

*Ganache* A combination of chocolate and heavy cream, melted and stirred together into an emulsion that can be used for dipping or coating candy centers, fruits, and cookies. Ganache also can be used as a glaze for cakes and pastries. The ratio of chocolate to cream determines how thick the final product will be.

*Ghee* Clarified butter used in Indian recipes. Authentic Indian ghee is often made from water buffalo butter and is sometimes flavored with spices.

*Glacéed fruit* Candied or crystallized fruit and fruit peels used in making fruitcakes, sweet breads, and other desserts.

*Granulated flour* Wheat flour processed to a fine, powdery texture. Also called sauce-and-gravy flour and quick-blending flour. Used primarily to thicken sauces and lightly coat ingredients.

*Jerk* Jerk can be used to refer to a method of cooking or a spice blend. Caribbean cooks apply a blend of habañero peppers, cinnamon, ginger, allspice, garlic, green onions, thyme, cloves, nutmeg, and brown sugar to meats, then slow-grill or smoke the victuals. The hot and sweet jerk seasoning can be a dry rub of dehydrated spices or a wet rub of fresh ingredients pureed with a small amount of oil. The exact recipe for jerk varies from island to island and cook to cook.

*Mortar and pestle* Frequently seen on a drugstore logo, the mortar and pestle is a device for grinding and smashing ingredients for use in recipes. A smooth, one-piece bowl (the mortar) is carved from wood or stone and a rounded-end, short, thick staff (the pestle) is used for pressing, breaking, and grinding ingredients. Spices, herb mixtures, garlic, and avocado are ingredients often prepared in a mortar and pestle.

*Muddle* To stir and press an ingredient to release fragrant oils and flavor. Muddling is often used in recipes involving mint, where the goal is to bruise the leaves slightly without creating the bitterness that would come from grinding or smashing. Muddling is achieved with a muddler, a thick stick with a round, flat end. Think of it as a flat-nosed pestle.

*Pizza peel* Sometimes called a baker's peel, it is a long-handled, very wide, flat wooden spatula used to remove pizza from a hot oven. Although some peels are made of metal, the wooden variety is best because it doesn't conduct heat readily.

*Rolling boil* A vigorous full boil in which large bubbles rise to the surface of a liquid.

*Scald* To heat a liquid just to the point of bubbling around the edges of the pan, but not boiling.

*Sear* To brown meat or other ingredients, but done quickly over high heat, usually in a skillet containing a minimal amount of fat.

*Separate* As it relates to eggs, *separate* means to divide the egg yolks from the egg whites and place each in containers.

*Sweat* To cook aromatic vegetables in a skillet, with or without a little oil, just until the ingredients begin to soften and give off liquid.

*Tapas* Literally, a cover, as in a small item to put on top of a glass of wine. However, the term has come to refer to a series of small dishes, bigger than a cocktail snack and smaller than an actual meal course. In Spain, where dinnertime is generally very late in the evening, restaurants and even homes serve tapas with wine or sherry to tide everyone over until the meal. In North America, *tapas* has come to refer to a meal made up of such small-plate dishes.

*Tent* To loosely cover an object by placing a triangle of foil over the top. Tenting can be used to keep a turkey breast from browning too quickly, or to cover a cooked dish in such a way as to allow steam to escape.

*Truss* To tie a bird or portion of meat with kitchen twine to either maintain a certain form as it cooks or secure the item on a spit.

*Whip* To beat vigorously; this can be done by hand with a whisk or with an electric mixer. Whipping, as opposed to mixing, is designed to lighten a batter or liquid by beating air into it.

*Wilt* To cook vegetables in a skillet until softened but not browned.

## Tips for Entertaining

Your keepsake cookbook may be filled with tales of grand soirees thrown by your garden club during the 1950s, or big outdoor picnics at your family farm. That said, it's a good bet that some of the readers of your cookbook will be from modern generations, many of whom find entertaining to be a daunting prospect. Here are a few guidelines they might find helpful.

- The quickest way to get hors d'oeuvres on the table is to build a cheese tray. Buy good-quality cheeses and select three to five different varieties. Include at least one firm, crumbly cheese like aged cheddar; one veined cheese like a blue cheese, Gorgonzola, or soft chèvre; and a buttery Camenbert or Brie. Add crackers or baguette rounds, a bowl of nuts, and a plate of grapes, sliced apples, or dried apricots, and you're set! (By the way, the same advice works for putting together an end-of-meal cheese course.)

- When buying wine for a cocktail party or reception, get three bottles of white for every two bottles of red. Unless you're serving oenophiles, look for wines that are somewhat light-bodied and relatively inexpensive. Save the expensive full-bodied wine for a dinner party.

- Five to six bottles of wine will serve ten people for a 1- to 1½-hour wine and cheese reception. For a dinner party, plan on one bottle of wine to accommodate two guests.

- One pound of good chocolate melted together with ⅔ cup heavy cream will provide an impressive dessert-table offering. Surround the chocolate with fresh strawberries, apple slices, biscotti, or shortbread cookies for dipping.

- Don't have a full bar? Don't run out and splurge on every liquor imaginable. Instead, come up with a signature before-dinner cocktail—classic martinis, pomegranate vodkatinis, margaritas, Sazerac slings, or some delicious concoction of your own—and whip up a pitcher. Serve that drink with hors d'oeuvres and move to wine and tea with dinner.

- Never underestimate the power of good, simple food. A roast chicken sprinkled with crushed garlic and rosemary tastes wonderful and makes your house smell heavenly. Likewise, only vegetarians can turn away from a good steak fresh off the grill. Add a vegetable, a salad, and a simple dessert, and you're done.

- When issuing dinner party invitations, find out if any of your guests have allergies or aversions to particular dishes. It's the hospitable and safe thing to do—no emergency room visits because you happen to make your hummus with a tablespoon of peanut butter instead of tahini.

**FAST FACTS:** From the sixteenth century on, plenty of religious orders have kept the monastery roof repaired by making spirits to sell to townspeople. Chartreuse, the green herbal elixir of France, is a product of the Carthusian monks. Bénédictine, the cognac-based liqueur, is the creation of Benedictine monks, although the product is now owned and bottled by Bacardi. (In deference to the liqueur's origins, the bottles have D.O.M. on the label, which stands for *Deo Optimo Maximo,* or "For our best, greatest God.") Of course, if you prefer to buy American, the Christian Brothers have been making brandy in California since the mid-1800s.

- If you're hosting a large gathering, don't be afraid to make it a potluck. You provide the main course—say, a roast turkey, a ham, or a choice of two lasagnas—as well as the libations, breads, plates, and utensils. Ask guests to bring salads, sides, and desserts.

- When guests bring wine as a host/hostess gift, you have a choice. You can open the bottle to share, or you can thank the giver profusely and set the bottle aside for another day. Don't feel that you have to open a bottle that either does not go with your meal plan, or—in the case of a really good bottle—will not stretch to provide a taste for each guest.

- Scented candles and potpourri are all well and good, but don't pick something too heavy or perfume-y to put near the dining room or kitchen. Aside from aggravating some guests' allergies, it will interfere with the smell, and therefore the enjoyment, of your meal. Stick with light citrus, apple, or herbal scents if you use anything at all. Woodsy or light cinnamon would be okay for a winter holiday party.

- Set an upbeat, mellow mood with music. Keep the Wagner and Marilyn Manson shelved and put on a classic crooner, vintage Motown, Mozart, jazz guitar, or New Orleans–style blues. Or, if you're hosting a theme party, pick music to match.

Remember, your friends are coming to see you, not your housekeeping prowess. Clean the bathroom and kitchen, fluff the pillows on the couch, turn the lights down in the rest of the house, and capitalize on the warm glow of candlelight.

## Spirited Offerings

If your cookbook offers party menus or party foods, you'll probably want to include a few recipes for freshly made cocktails, particularly if your audience includes younger-set adults who believe good drinks come from a prepackaged mix, bottle, or slushy tap.

It's always helpful to have some idea of how to make the old-school favorites, the imbibers' equivalent of comfort food. Those recipes appear first, followed by some trendy frozen fare. Feel free to include these in your book or adapt them to your own tastes.

Encourage your readers to skip packaged mixes and bottled mix concentrates. Cocktails made with fresh or frozen fruits and fruit juices, freshly opened bottled seltzer or tonic, and decent spirits taste best.

## Classic Cocktails

### Whiskey Sour

2 ounces blended whiskey

1 tablespoon fresh lemon juice

½ teaspoon confectioners' sugar

1 maraschino cherry

1 lemon slice

Pour whiskey, lemon juice, and sugar into a cocktail shaker filled with ice. Shake vigorously and strain into a whiskey sour glass. Garnish with cherry and lemon slice.

### Manhattan

3 ounces rye whiskey (or bourbon)

½ ounce vermouth

1 dash Angostura bitters

1 maraschino cherry

Pour ingredients, except for the cherry, into a cocktail glass filled with ice. Stir to blend. Strain into a chilled, stemmed cocktail glass. Garnish with cherry.

### Sidecar

2 ounces good cognac

1 ounce Cointreau or Grand Marnier

1 ounce fresh lemon juice

Coarse sugar

Pour the first three ingredients into a cocktail shaker filled with ice. Shake vigorously. Coat the rim of a martini glass with sugar. Strain drink into the glass and serve.

**FAST FACTS:** Bourbon whiskey and Tennessee whiskey are both American-born products and both corn-based spirits, but aficionados will be quick to tell you they're two different things. Bourbon originated in Bourbon County, Kentucky, and while it can be produced anywhere in the United States, it must be 51 percent corn mash and it must be aged in new, charred oak casks. Tennessee whiskey is sold only in certain counties in Tennessee, and the corn mash distillate must be filtered through maple charcoal before it is aged in casks.

## The Aviation

2 ounces high-quality dry gin
¾ ounce maraschino liqueur
¾ ounce fresh lemon juice
A few drops crème de violette (optional)
Twist of lemon peel

Pour ingredients into a shaker filled with ice. Shake thoroughly and strain into a chilled cocktail glass. Garnish with a twist of lemon peel.

## Tom Collins

4 ounces gin
2 tablespoons fresh lemon juice
1 tablespoon sugar syrup
Club soda

Combine gin, juice, and syrup in a tall glass. Stir well. Add a handful of cracked ice to the glass and top it off with club soda.

## Bacardi Cocktail

1¾ ounces light rum
1 ounce fresh lime juice
½ teaspoon sugar syrup
Dash grenadine syrup

Pour ingredients into a cocktail shaker filled with ice. Shake well and strain into a chilled cocktail glass.

## Bellini

½ peeled peach, pureed
5 ounces cold, dry sparkling wine

Pour peach puree in a champagne flute. Pour sparkling wine into the glass and serve.

*Note:* 1 ounce peach schnapps can be used in place of the peach.

## The Millionaire Rum Cocktail

*1½ ounces dark rum*
*¾ ounce apricot brandy*
*¾ ounce sloe gin*
*¾ ounce fresh pomegranate juice*
*¾ ounce fresh lime juice*
*Dash of pomegranate syrup or grenadine syrup*
*Lime wedge*

Pour ingredients into a cocktail shaker filled with ice. Shake thoroughly. Strain into a chilled cocktail glass. Garnish with a wedge of lime.

## Scotch Milk Punch

*2 ounces Scotch whisky*
*6 ounces milk*
*1 teaspoon confectioners' sugar*
*Nutmeg*

Combine whisky, milk, and sugar in a cocktail shaker filled with ice. Shake well. Strain into a tall glass and sprinkle with nutmeg.

*Note:* To make "butterscotch" punch, substitute ½ ounce Drambuie, 1 ounce Scotch, and ½ ounce Cointreau for the 2 ounces of Scotch in the recipe.

## Mint Julep

*6 mint leaves*
*2 teaspoons confectioners' sugar*
*2 teaspoons water*
*2 ounces bourbon*
*Cracked ice*

Chill a silver tumbler or julep glass. Add mint leaves, sugar, and water to the glass and muddle with a spoon until mint leaves are pressed and fragrant. Fill the glass halfway with cracked ice and add the bourbon. Let stand for flavors to mingle, then add more cracked ice. Sip slowly through a straw.

## Palm Beach Cocktail

1½ ounces gin
½ ounce sweet vermouth
1 ounce fresh pink grapefruit juice
1 tablespoon sugar syrup
Grapefruit peel

Combine ingredients in a cocktail shaker filled with ice. Shake thoroughly and strain into a prechilled cocktail glass. Garnish with grapefruit peel.

## Cuba Libre

1½ ounces rum
Juice of ½ lime
Cold Coca-Cola
Lime wedges

Combine rum and lime in a tall glass, add ice, and pour Coke to fill. Garnish with lime wedges.

## Singapore Sling

1½ ounces gin
½ ounce cherry brandy
Juice of 1 lemon
Cracked ice
Cold club soda or lemonade
Maraschino cherries and orange slice for garnish

Pour gin, brandy, and lemon juice into a cocktail shaker filled with cracked ice. Shake well. Strain into a tall glass, fill with club soda or lemonade, and garnish with cherries and orange slice. Sip through a straw.

## Daiquiri

*1½ ounces light rum*
*1 tablespoon sugar syrup*
*Juice of two limes*
*Cracked ice*

Combine all ingredients in a cocktail shaker. Shake vigorously and strain into a glass.

## Margarita

*1½ ounces tequila*
*½ ounce Triple Sec*
*Juice of one lime*
*Cracked ice*
*Salt*

Pour tequila, Triple Sec, and lime juice into a shaker filled with cracked ice. Shake, then strain into a glass with a salted rim. (To salt rim, moisten edge with lime juice and dip into a layer of salt.)

**FAST FACTS:** The first home-grown distilled spirit of North America was tequila. Produced from the 1600s in the Mexican region of Jalisco, the spirit is a direct descendant of a fermented beverage made by the Aztecs using the fruits of the blue agave plant. Spanish settlers took the agave plant and began to apply European brandy-making techniques to create a more refined drink. The first tequila showed up in the United States in the late 1800s.

## Long Island Iced Tea

*1 ounce each vodka, tequila, rum, gin, and Triple Sec*
*1½ ounces sweet and sour mix*
*Splash cola*
*Lemon wedges*

Combine alcohol, sweet and sour mix, and cola in a cocktail shaker filled with ice. Give one good shake, then strain into a tall glass filled with ice. Garnish with lemon wedges.

## Gin, Vodka, or Rum and Tonic

1½ ounces gin, rum, or vodka
Cold tonic
Lime or lemon wedge

Pour alcohol of choice (gin is the classic) over ice in a tall glass. Add tonic to fill. Stir gently and garnish with a lime or lemon wedge.

## Frozen Cocktails

### Speed-Scratch Frozen Margaritas

1 6-ounce can frozen limeade concentrate
6 ounces tequila
2 ounces Triple Sec
Cracked ice
Coarse salt
Lime wedges

1. Empty frozen limeade concentrate into a 5-cup blender container. Refill the limeade can with tequila and pour into the blender. Fill can one-third full with Triple Sec and add to blender.

2. Pack blender with cracked ice and pulse until mixture has combined and ice is well chopped. Then blend on high speed until mixture is smooth.

3. Moisten the rims of four margarita glasses with water or lime juice, then dip rims into a bowl of coarse salt. Divide frozen margarita mixture among the four glasses and garnish with lime wedges.

MAKES 4 SERVINGS.

### Speed-Scratch Frozen Daiquiris

1 6-ounce can frozen limeade, orange juice, or pineapple juice concentrate
6 ounces white rum
2 ounces Triple Sec

*Cracked ice*
*Turbinado or coarse sugar*
*Lime, orange, or pineapple wedges*

1.  Empty frozen drink concentrate into a 5-cup blender container. Refill the can with rum and pour into the blender. Fill can one-third full with Triple Sec and add to blender.

2.  Pack blender with cracked ice and pulse until mixture has combined and ice is well chopped. Then blend on high speed until mixture is smooth.

3.  Moisten the rims of four martini glasses with water or fruit juice, then dip rims into a bowl of sugar. Divide frozen daiquiri mixture among the four glasses and garnish with fruit wedges.

MAKES 4 SERVINGS.

## Frozen Hard Lemonade

*1 6-ounce can frozen lemonade concentrate*
*6 ounces bourbon*
*2 ounces brandy*
*Cracked ice*
*Stemmed cherries*

1.  Empty frozen drink concentrate into a 5-cup blender container. Refill the can with bourbon and pour into the blender. Fill can one-third full with brandy and add to blender.

2.  Pack blender with cracked ice and pulse until mixture has combined and ice is well chopped. Then blend on high speed until mixture is smooth.

3.  Moisten the rims of four martini glasses with water or lemon juice, then dip rims into a bowl of sugar. Divide frozen mixture among glasses and garnish with cherries.

MAKES 4 SERVINGS.

## Sangria Slush

2 cups red table wine
1 ounce brandy
½ cup mandarin orange sections
1 tablespoon sugar
Cracked ice
Cinnamon sticks
Orange slices

1. Pour wine, brandy, orange sections, and sugar into a 5-cup blender container. Pulse to combine.

2. Fill container with cracked ice and pulse until ice is well chopped. Then blend at high speed until mixture is smooth. Pour into four large wine glasses and garnish with cinnamon sticks and orange slices.

MAKES 4 SERVINGS.

**FAST FACTS:** Opening your own brewpub is a risky business, mostly because the restaurant business is fraught with pitfalls. However, if you always wanted to have your own beer brand, that might be within reach. It takes $500,000 to $800,000 to start a small microbrewery and if you're good at selling your wares to restaurants and retailers, you could become a beer magnate in your own town!

## Frozen Cosmopolitans

3 ounces citrus-flavored vodka
1 ounce Cointreau
4 ounces frozen cranberry juice concentrate
Juice of 2 limes
3 cups cracked ice

Pour vodka, Cointreau, cranberry juice concentrate, and lime juice into a blender container. Add cracked ice and pulse until ice is well chopped. Then blend on high speed until mixture is smooth. Pour into two martini glasses.

MAKES 2 SERVINGS.

# Tapping Memory Banks: Gathering Stories

When my memoir cookbook *Roux Memories: A Cajun-Creole Love Story with Recipes* came out, I expected my mother to be pleased. After all, I was finally coming home, gastronomically speaking, to the cuisines that nourished our extended family for generations. I had already written several cookbooks, all of which she expressed pride over. But this book—which includes South Louisiana family stories, photos, and recipes—would really speak to her.

Mom's reaction was everything I had hoped and expected it would be. However, I didn't expect the reaction I got from the rest of the family—and by "rest," I mean the first, second, and third cousins, and people I hadn't seen or spoken with in decades who called, e-mailed, and came to visit. Friends from high school came to my book signings, and strangers wanted to talk to me about the people, locations, and ingredients in the book. One woman told me that my family's vintage photos mimicked the ones in her own albums. I was both flattered and stunned.

A cousin tried to explain the support. "You didn't just tell your story," she said. "You told our story too. You've touched a lot of people."

The point of telling you about my experience is this: Your keepsake cookbook, however expansive or concise it may be, will touch people. It will bring them together to celebrate the flavors and the journeys that make your table unique. Because you're not just arranging a bunch of recipes. You're telling stories. How you bring those stories to the page depends on the type of cookbook you're crafting and your own creative preferences.

Family cookbooks offer the perfect venue for small recollections, favorite sayings, and even substantial essays. Special-occasion cookbooks can be filled with narrowly focused memories, advice, and menu or decorating ideas. Group cookbooks draw on the common memories of an organization or institution.

To add those pieces to your cookbook, you have to scan your own memory in an orderly way and be willing to interview friends, family members, and sometimes even strangers. This chapter provides tools to tap those memories and enhance your keepsake. You'll also get tips for writing and presenting memories without feeling like you're back in composition class.

## Your Memoir Cookbook

You already know that the connections between food and feelings, and between food and memory, are strong. If you're a born writer or a dedicated journal-keeper, you probably have recollections of holidays and meals already recorded somewhere. That trove could be the inspiration for the short essays that will make your cookbook a food memoir.

Even if you don't think of yourself as a writer, it isn't difficult to add personal essays to the mix of ingredients in your keepsake cookbook. You just need to put yourself in the right frame of mind. Think back to the first Thanksgiving dinner you helped prepare, the temperature in and out of the kitchen, the conversations punctuated by the clang of pots and pans, the aromas wafting through the house. Consider your favorite type of birthday cake and the birthday rituals your family observed during your childhood. Or maybe you remember teaching your son or daughter to make cookies, using a recipe handed down from your grandmother.

Think of a food-related scene and ask yourself these questions:

- Who was cooking?

- What was the occasion?

- Where did it take place? Who was visiting?

- What dishes were on the menu? Which was your favorite?

- What was the topic of conversation?

- What did you learn that day?

- Who or what made you laugh? Or cry?

- What or who from that scene do you miss most?

These simple yet open-ended questions can trigger a brainstorm of memories. Maybe you were a small child in this scenario and it's the first memory you have of your mother and grandmother cooking together. Maybe your grandfather walked into the kitchen with field-dressed ducks and your grandmother shooed him to the utility room sink. Maybe you overheard two aunts talking about a time when your mother was the belle of the ball. Or when your grandfather lied about his age to join the army. Maybe it was the day you helped your mother cook and learned something about yourself.

If words don't naturally flow, or if you want to hold the memory for writing later in the process, make notes using a format that will help you keep track of things you want to include and their significance.

For example:

- **Date:** 1962

- **Occasion, place:** My 7th birthday, at the house on Shrewsbury Court. At the kitchen table.

- **People:** Mama, Grandma, Colin, Brett, and Daddy

- **Food:** My red velvet birthday cake, ice cream from the Borden's store. Mom was grilling French bread for hamburger Po-Boys.

- **I learned:** I was going to have a little brother or sister soon.

- **I felt:** I knew my prayers had been answered because I so wanted a sister to play with.

Another approach would be recipe-specific. Select a few of your favorite recipes. For each recipe, answer a set of prompts. For example:

- **The food was:** cheesecake

- **The predominant flavor of this dish is:** tart vanilla cream

- **The first time I tasted this, I was:** at a neighbor's house, and I was 10 years old.

- **When I eat this dish, I remember:** how, the first time I had it, I wanted more, begged Mom to make one. She didn't like cheesecake, but she made it. I snuck into the refrigerator and ate half of it myself. I got sick. Mom was so astonished (and felt sorry for me) that she didn't get mad.

- **When I cook this, I think about:** the fact that cheesecake still tastes best when you eat it with a spoon from the refrigerator. Just not all of it.

**FAST FACTS:** Ambrosia may have been the mythical food of the gods in ancient Greece, but the well-loved concoction of oranges, pineapple, and shredded coconut is a product of the American South. Food historians place the creation of the dish at the end of the nineteenth century, coinciding with the availability of dried coconut. The cherries, marshmallows, and other goodies? Definitely later additions.

## Writing Your Essay

An essay is an expression of personal evolution. Keepsake cookbook essays obviously draw on food-related memories to describe a pivotal time or to make a point about life, about transitions. The essays can be short, long, funny, sweet, or poignant, but each one should have rich descriptions and a sense of movement. Something should happen during the essay, even if it's just a change in your view of certain things, or in your ability to duplicate the flavors in question.

Fully fleshed-out essays can be used to accent different segments of your book, including chapters on types of dishes, chapters or photos related to different eras, or collections of memorabilia related to specific locations. For example, my memoir cookbook *Roux Memories* was divided into fairly traditional recipe categories. Each chapter of the book got a full-fledged essay, while individual recipes got shorter anecdotes or notes.

The chapter on sweets began with this remembrance of an incident involving my grandmother.

### Grandma and the *Traiteur*

*My grandmother would have thrown herself in front of a bus to keep me safe from harm. So when she heard the knock on the farmhouse door, she took the time to unplug the hot iron from the wall, wrap the cord, and hold it by the handle to keep me—then a rambunctious six-year-old—from pulling the iron off the ironing board.*

*I missed that entire precautionary process. I heard the knock and came running in from the back porch to say hello to the "Butane man" who delivered cooking and heating fuel to the farm. I ran straight to the front door and pushed into Grandma's apron and peered around her hip. Somehow I raised my hand and smashed a finger squarely into the hot iron.*

*I'll spare you all the painful details. Let's suffice it to say that I screamed. And screamed. And screamed. Grandma cried. The Butane man offered to go out and buy me an ice cream. Then Grandma pulled it together and found a towel to wrap my hand. We walked across the dirt drive to visit the family that worked the farm—who were actually cousins. Among their seven children was one son in medical school who happened to be home. He applied first aid to my charred finger and whispered instructions to Grandma. The younger kids tried to cheer me up by showing me a bunch of just-hatched chickens in the yard.*

*Then Grandma told me to walk back to the house and get in the car. She helped me into the front passenger seat before tucking herself behind the wheel of her giant, green, column-shifting Chevrolet. As the dust cloud lifted behind the car, I started to whine. "I don't want to go to the doctor," I said. She told me not to worry, that we were going to someone like a doctor, but not really. She promised it wouldn't hurt.*

*After about 2 miles on gravel roads, we pulled into a farmyard with a white two-story house next to a grove of oak trees. There was a swing set in the front yard and plenty of tricycles, baby carriages, and other toys strewn around. Before Grandma turned off the engine, a bunch of children ran from the house and sur-rounded the car. I didn't know them, but they seemed very happy to see us. One of the older girls put her arm around me and we walked toward the front porch with Grandma following behind.*

*Then I saw him. The girl's father was a tall, thin man with thick, curly, silver-streaked black hair. He took Grandma's hand and spoke softly to her in French. The only words I understood were "la petite" and "malheureux." He looked in my direc-tion and gave me the kindest, gentlest smile I'd ever seen. "Vien chere," he said. I stared at him like a deer caught in the headlights. "He can help you," said one of the boys, pointing to my bandaged finger.*

*I walked into the house with an entourage of five or six children. The nice man told us to wait downstairs. I looked around anxiously, but nobody seemed worried. There were no sympathy stares. When he called me to come upstairs, only the older daughter came with me. She held my undamaged hand and told me I had to be very quiet and not talk to her father while he was helping me. I nodded.*

*We entered a small room where an altar had been set up. There was a bowl of some kind of dried leaves or flowers, a linen towel, a vial of water, a crucifix, and several candles. The man put my hand on the towel and lifted it slightly. He closed his eyes, and I could see his lips move. He crossed two unlit tapers and held them over my hand, then put them aside and put his hand on my head. All the while he seemed to be in a trance, whispering prayers I couldn't understand.*

*When it was over, he put his hands on my shoulders, smiled, and turned me toward the door. The older daughter closed the door behind us and escorted me downstairs. There Grandma was chatting with the lady of the house and the other kids were watching cartoons on TV. Eventually, the nice man joined us and the conversation turned to the weather and other normal things. By the time we left, my finger didn't hurt quite as much.*

*Since I didn't really know what had happened there, I never spoke of it to anyone for a long time. Years later, after Grandma had died, my mother and I were watching a documentary on healers in different cultures. There was a segment on Cajun traiteurs (male) and traiteuses (female). It told of how Cajun healers had to be asked for help before they could intervene, that they could never ask for money, and they could only channel healing from God. That part was stressed—that a traiteur might use folk medicine, but the gift and its healing power come from God.*

*I asked Mom if she remembered the time I'd been burned by an iron. "Of course," she said. "Grandma felt so, so bad about that and—" I interrupted her. "Your mother took me to a traiteur." Mom stared at me as if I'd told her Grandma had made me slaughter a hog for dinner.*

*"But Grandma wasn't superstitious," she whispered. "I guess she just didn't know what else to do."*

*Probably so. She took me to both a doctor and a faith healer, and she also did the one thing that cheered me more than either of their treatments. When we got back to the farmhouse, Grandma took me to the back room where the giant chest freezer hummed. We pulled out cartons of ice cream, sat on low benches, and just started eating wonderful homemade ice cream out of the containers. The frozen sweet cream soothed any discomfort I had.*

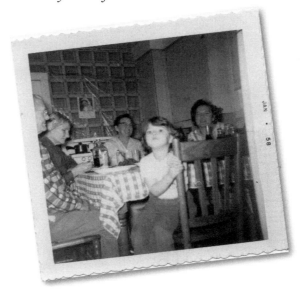

## Grandma's Homemade Ice Cream

*2 cups sugar*
*1½ tablespoons cornstarch*
*3 cups cold milk*
*1 cup half-and-half*
*2 eggs*
*4 teaspoons vanilla*
*2 cups heavy cream*

1.  In a large saucepan, whisk together sugar and cornstarch until well blended. Add cold milk and whisk until smooth. Place pan over medium heat and slowly add half-and-half. Whisk until sugar and cornstarch are completely dissolved.

2.  Place eggs in a blender with a few tablespoons of cold milk or cream. Pulse until well mixed.

3.  Keep stirring ice cream mixture with a whisk or wooden spoon until liquid is scalding hot, but not boiling. Turn blender with eggs on low and slowly add a large ladleful of hot liquid into eggs, then pour tempered eggs from blender into the saucepan. Whisk quickly and constantly until egg mixture is blended into ice cream.

4.  Keep cooking and stirring until mixture just begins to bubble. Remove from heat. Stir in vanilla and heavy cream. Allow mixture to cool in pan, then strain into a pitcher and chill in the refrigerator until ready to use.

5.  Freeze according to ice cream maker instructions.

MAKES 10 SERVINGS.

*Note:* This recipe can be used as a base for many different ice cream flavors. If you're adding sweetened fruit or sweet syrups to the mix (or if you prefer a less sweet vanilla ice cream), reduce sugar to 1½ cups.

*Source: Roux Memories: A Cajun-Creole Love Story with Recipes* (Lyons Press, 2010)

This particular essay tapped into a long-dormant memory of mine. My grandmother, who passed away before my children were born, was an important person in my life and my food memories. This essay conveys something about the relationship between me and my grandmother. But it also does something else: It tells about the unique tradition of the Cajun faith healer and gives some context for my interaction with this part of my family culture.

Other writers in other cookbooks might want to recall an incident while sailing with Dad, learning to churn butter with a great-aunt, shopping for school clothes with Mom, learning to take care of a grandparent with dementia, or working at a soup kitchen as part of a group project. The important thing is that your essay fits the theme and audience for your book, and that your recollections have a generosity of spirit. That means no blatantly unkind depictions of the relatives, friends, and colleagues mentioned! When you tell a funny story, you want the people involved to be laughing the hardest.

## Other Options

If you're not up for essay writing, don't worry. You can give your book personality and flavor without having to write a treatise. Instead, punctuate your book with similarly formatted profiles of people or events. Let's say your grandmother was a horrible cook. But she made every minute you spent with her magical—playing dress-up and board games and building puppet theaters. She had one dish that she prepared every time you visited, because you loved it and because it was the only thing she did well. It wasn't until you grew up that you learned that she made her "famous" macaroni and cheese from a box, with one secret ingredient. So, your profile of her might look like this:

*Granny Annie Mason*
*Born:* *March 3, 1938*
*Hometown:* *Jacksonville, Florida*
*Occupation:* *Retired speech teacher*
*Mother to:* *Mike Mason and Betty Mason Smith*
*Loves:* *Musical theater, Elvis, proper enunciation, her six grandchildren, and her Lhasa-poo Buddy*
*Favorite saying:* *I love my stove. It's as shiny as the day I bought it!*

*Favorite pastime: Putting on plays with grandchildren, shopping garage sales, forwarding e-mail jokes to family and friends. Yelling at the politicians on TV.*
*Favorite dish: Fried catfish from The Shack, with hush puppies.*
*Culinary claim to fame: Adds half a small jar of pimiento cheese, real butter, and heavy cream to mac 'n' cheese from a box and calls it Macaroni au Frommage. Also very generous with caramel sauce and whipped cream on ice cream.*

For a group cookbook, you could include short, structured profiles of group members. For a commemorative cookbook, the profiles could focus on all the past presidents of the club, the people who have been members for twenty-five years, or even people who have been helped by the club. You could ask dear friends or acquaintances of the people featured to write the profiles. This would give the book a generous, celebratory feel, rather than the kind of clinical résumé accounting one would find in an annual report.

An even easier alternative—which works very well with large groups—is to have each person submit a quote, related to either the theme of the club or the recipes inside. For the twenty-fifth anniversary of the River Ranch Rose Society, you might see boxes featuring quotes like this:

> My heart is still in the Lone Star State. So every time I see this
> Republic of Texas yellow rose bush blooming in my garden, it makes
> me smile. The best part is that it blooms almost year-round here!
> Jeannie Stahl
> Member since 1997

The quotes could be interspersed with photos of award-winning blooms, lists of competition winners, and individual members' tips on growing and displaying roses. The recipe aspect of the book might take on a garden tea theme, with members submitting recipes for cookies, small cakes, sandwiches, biscuits, and beverages.

For a supper club's cookbook, each host or hostess could relate how he or she came up with menus or comment on a fellow club member's amazing dish. Or, for a Temple sisterhood cookbook, each member could offer her favorite food memory from the weekly Kiddush table at the synagogue, or a memory from the annual Women's Seder.

Cookbooks can also chronicle events. They can include photos and extended explanations that tell of a travel club's exploits, a community center's physical evolution (the year of the playground, the year the pool went in, the year we added a real basketball court), or an extended family's migration from Naples, Italy, to Sonoma, California.

**FAST FACTS:** Cooks in both the northern and southern United States make cornbread. However, southern cornbread traditionally is an unsweetened, thin, crisp-edged affair while northern cooks add more leavening and sugar to the mix. Northern-style cornbread and corn muffins are more cakelike, with a lighter crumb and sweeter flavor.

I love the process of personalizing gift cookbooks, because the theme is generally very focused and fun. A great idea for a baby shower keepsake cookbook would be for each person attending to contribute three things: a recipe for something easy to fix, a photo of himself or herself as a baby, and a bit of parenting advice. The end result would be a relatively small book full of carefully chosen recipes, helpful ideas, and sweet pictures.

A wedding shower or anniversary cookbook might be filled with little vignettes and pictures from the weddings of family members and friends, plus recollections of funny marriage advice that contributors may have been given. For example, an uncle might supply a photo of himself being fed wedding cake by his bride, with this quote:

The best marriage advice I ever got was to say "I love you" every night, and to always compliment her cooking . . . even if I know she bought it already made!
Uncle Sam McCall

## Interviewing Family and Friends

If your book is a chronicle of your own memories, the questions at the beginning of this chapter will help you flesh out those recollections and put them in usable form. Pictures, old scrapbooks, letters, and music—not to mention cooking and eating—can help put you in a memoir-writing mood as well.

However, if your concept requires contributions from other family members or organization members, you have several options. You can identify those individuals who have the information, history, and cooking secrets you most wish to unlock, then actually spend time with them. Invite them to tea, pull up a chair in their kitchen while they cook, or pick up the phone.

Or you can create an interview/questionnaire that can be e-mailed or mailed to a wide range of folks. In the case of a family cookbook, you may wish to do both—spend time with Grandma and take notes while she's sharing heretofore unwritten recipes, then send an e-mail questionnaire to the cousins and second cousins who are somewhat tech-savvy.

When interviewing elderly relatives in person, keep in mind that while they're probably happy to spend time and chat, they may not perceive of themselves as "keepers" of culinary history. Their experience with meals and recipes likely owes more to necessity than creativity. There are some dishes they'll be surprised to hear that you recall fondly and some they'll be surprised to hear that you don't know how to make.

Start the interview gently, by asking specifics about a particular recipe: "You always make the best pot roast. How do you get it so tender? What do you do to make the gravy so dark and rich?" or "How do you get your piecrust so flaky? Do you use any particular kind of apples in your pie? Why does your cinnamon taste so spicy?"

The answers to such simple queries may give details you can use, or prompt other questions. When I asked my husband's grandmother those questions, I learned that her piecrust was always made with cold lard, the apples were always from the late-fall harvest from the orchard two towns over, and the cinnamon was freshly ground from whole cinnamon sticks. This led to discussions of her father helping to plant the orchard in question and she and her sister getting to pick all the apples they could reach every October of their childhood. The conversation gave me wonderful stories to tell, and it also helped me create a more accurate written recipe for her pie.

Once you get the conversation going around one or more specific dishes, you can expand the interview territory with questions like these:

- What was your favorite dish that your mother made? Did she teach you to make it?

- Who taught you to cook most of the things you make now?

- What did your family eat when money was tight? What ingredients were most plentiful in your house?

**FAST FACTS:** Do you find yourself struggling with uneven, cracked cake layers and loaves? Check your oven temperature. Too-high temperatures cause fast-rising and cracked cake tops.

- What countries did your parents or grandparents come from? What foods did they make from the "old country"? How did they celebrate holidays?

- What was the first meal you made for your spouse-to-be (or what was the first meal made for you by your spouse-to-be)?

- What recipes and customs came into your life when you got married? Who taught you to make the new dishes? Did you like eating them?

- When you wanted to impress someone, what dish did you make?

- How have your tastes changed over the years?

- What is your favorite entree? Your favorite dessert?

- What dish did your children (or my mother/my father) love most when they were growing up?

Those questions can be modified for tapping the memories of long-standing members of a group or association. For large groups, or for a cookbook including input from extended family members, an e-mail questionnaire might be more efficient. Make up your own or choose a selection of questions from the following list.

- What is your favorite dish? Who makes the best version?

- What dish would friends say is your specialty?

- Where did you learn to cook?

- What is your favorite childhood food memory?

- What restaurants did your family frequent when you were a child? What do you remember about that?

- What were the biggest food holidays for your family? What dishes were always on the menu? Who did the cooking?

- What special dish that your parents made do you now cook for your family or friends?

- What kind of birthday cake did you have as a child?

- What ethnic dishes appeared most often in your childhood home?

- What is your first memory involving food? Who was there? What was the occasion?

- Did you ever catch or kill your own dinner? Who taught you to fish or hunt? Did you ever grow your own food?

- What's your favorite unusual snack?

- If you could eat only one food for the rest of your life, what would it be?

- What dish do you always have trouble preparing?

- What's the funniest kitchen disaster that ever happened to you?

- Did you ever cook for your pets? What treats do they like?

**FAST FACTS:** The first American-made china used in the White House was ordered during the administration of Woodrow Wilson. Some 1,700 pieces of the gold-banded china arrived in 1918, at a cost of $16,000.

**FAST FACTS:** Think you have problems serving a large dinner party? The State Dining Room at the White House can hold 140 dinner guests.

- Did you every consider being a vegetarian?

- What did you usually order when you went to restaurants with a date?

- What did you prepare, or where did you have dinner, when you first dined with your future spouse?

- Who is your food hero?

- Are you a natural cook or a recipe cook?

- Name five relatives (or group members) you consider to be great cooks, and name your favorite dish that they prepare.

- What description of food or a meal in literature got your attention?

- What kind of china, flatware, and crystal do you own? Does your "good china" come from a family member or did you get it as wedding gifts or buy it yourself? Did you pick the pattern?

- What is your favorite kind of dinner party? A buffet, a sit-down, a barbecue, a boil . . . ? How do you prefer to entertain and be entertained?

These questions relate to food and cooking, but you might also add some questions related to group history or genealogy. If each person you query answers only one question in an interesting or unique way, your cookbook will be richer for it!

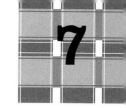

# Collecting and Taking Photographs:
# Picturing Your Memories

First-class food photography—those culinary pinup shots that make foodies sigh—requires a small cadre of professionals, including a chef, a food stylist, an experienced photographer, and one or more assistants. In addition, those professionals need top-flight equipment: cameras, lenses, lighting, and settings.

Maybe you are such a photographer, in which case your keepsake cookbook will undoubtedly be studded with jewel-like photographs of finished dishes. Or maybe you have a really good hobby photographer on your group cookbook committee. With a few helpers, he or she might be able to turn out some great food shots.

But even if your photography skills are limited to snapping your kids' birthday parties and other life-cycle events, you can still put together a visually compelling keepsake. Mix vintage, special occasion, and casual photos from your personal or group collection with photos of dinner parties, picnics, and other food events, plus a few decent amateur food photos, and you'll be in great shape.

In this chapter we'll go over some tips for taking good cookbook photos, and for selecting existing pictures to enhance your book.

## Food Photography for Non-Professional Photographers

As a food writer, I've worked with a number of excellent food photographers over the years. I consider their work to be high craftsmanship, and in some cases, art. Standing by their sides while they frame and shoot has been both a blessing and a curse. A curse because I compare my amateur photos to their professional efforts and always come up short. A blessing because I've learned a few things that have made my food photos much, much better.

Here are a few of the tips and techniques I've picked up. Follow these and I think you'll have a good selection of attractive food photos for your keepsake cookbook.

## Keep It Simple

Unless you're going for a section-divider photo of a dinner party buffet or a holiday feast, in which case the theme is abundance and not a particular recipe, limit the number of items in your photograph. A single muffin, a perfect poached pear drizzled with caramel sauce, or a white bowl of chili garnished with a few slices of avocado and a soupçon of sour cream will have much more impact than a busy place setting with a lot of different dishes.

Don't underestimate the visual impact of raw ingredients. A single red bell pepper, a basket of multicolor fingerling potatoes, a cluster of tomatoes on the vine, or a quartered pineapple with the crown intact will photograph beautifully and give your photo a sense of the potential of just-picked ingredients.

## Light It Up

Yes, you can use your automatic camera setting. But you still need to make sure the star of your picture is well-lighted. One of the reasons so many food photos are shot, improbably, on outdoor tables or blankets is because natural light is very kind to most subjects. A slice of pound cake on a medium blue plate, nicely dusted with a touch of confectioners' sugar and kissed with a few fresh raspberries, will look beautiful sitting atop a white tablecloth on a poolside table, or directly on a weathered-wood picnic table, when shot in the mid-morning sunlight.

**FAST FACTS:** Farmed catfish can be found at most supermarkets today. However, old-time catfish lovers will find that farm-raised cats have a much milder flavor than their wild-caught cousins. Wild catfish take on the flavors of whatever they find to eat in their freshwater homes. Farmed catfish are fed a controlled diet for consistency of flavor and texture.

Barring access to a good outdoor backdrop, plan to use desk lamps or shaded overhead lights to create an attractive, shadow-neutral environment for your photo. You'll need at least two movable lights, possibly three, to get the effect you want. Arrange the lights so the primary lighting falls diagonally from above and behind the dish. Use the side lights to erase unwanted shadows. A makeshift frame filled with gauze, waxed paper, or tissue paper can be used to diffuse the light. You can use a large embroidery hoop or needlepoint frame for the job, or make your own frame with dowels or cardboard.

If you plan to shoot a lot of food photos, you can buy a portable popup "studio" for photographing small objects. It's essentially a tabletop-size translucent tent with lights; the cost ranges from $100 to $200. Or you can make your own by cutting windows in the sides and bottom of a cardboard box. Cover the windows with gauze or some other translucent material. Put the box on its side and situate desk lamps around the box. The gauze will diffuse the lamplight and give you an evenly lit stage for your dish.

## Get in Style

Food styling is at the heart of great-looking food photos. Make the scene look as appetizing as possible before you start to snap pictures. Think symmetry, accents, and color contrast. If you're planning to shoot a beautiful whole cake, think in terms of a sleek glass or homey ceramic cake stand to showcase the cake. Place the stand on a tablecloth that offers nice contrast, maybe with an ornate silver cake server angled at the base. Shooting a coffee cake or something with interesting interior detail—say, a cinnamon strudel—requires a nicely cut slice on plate, possibly with the whole cake in the background, and a fork or napkin in the foreground. Even a plate of fresh black-eyed peas can look beautiful when placed in a scalloped, shallow milk-glass bowl with a triangle of cornbread balanced on the side and a spoonful of minced peppers or a sprig of parsley at the center.

**FAST FACTS:** In the New World, wild boars weren't always wild. These large, tusked pigs were domesticated by Europeans, who then brought them to their colonies on ships. As once-captive boars began to escape, they found comfy homes in the swamps and forests of the land. Since boars easily interbreed with domestic hogs, some escaped domestic pigs became part of the wild boar family tree. Today American boars are both hunted in the wild and raised on farms.

If you have a beautiful background picked out—for instance, a lush garden or a lovely mosaic tile backsplash—by all means go with it. But don't be afraid to just hang a white sheet or stand a section of black cardboard behind the dish being photographed. A neutral background puts the focus on the dish rather than the environment. Whatever you do, you don't want a lot of mundane visuals—like the kitchen sink, a messy desk, or a refrigerator—to be in the photo.

## Gild the Lily . . . or the Roast Pork

Keep a spray bottle of vegetable oil, or a bowl of oil and a pastry brush, on hand when you're shooting pictures of food. Savory foods and produce can look lackluster or dull in photos. A little spritz or light coating of oil can make cooked foods or cut produce look more colorful and appetizing. If you feel the need to have steam rising in the photo, a cup of boiling water or wet cotton balls heated in the microwave—carefully hidden behind the food—can give the wisps of smoke you desire.

### Get Down with It

Shoot from a low angle. Most amateur photographers stand next to the plate of food and shoot from above. For most dishes, that isn't the most flattering vantage, nor does it give a sense of the finished dish. Instead, shoot with the dish at or slightly below eye level, which gives a full view of the dish or the portion being photographed. The exception to this rule is when you want a flat, two-dimensional photo of the ingredients in a bowl or pot. For that shot, you'll need to stand atop a chair or ladder and shoot straight down to get the right perspective.

### Crop and Cut

Your food photo should be a close-up glamour shot. But even if the picture is well focused, don't be afraid to crop the edges of the photo to make the end result look more dramatic. A shallow oven-safe bowl of blueberry cobbler with a browned sweet biscuit on top might look perfect with the edges of the bowl showing. However, a dish of fresh blueberries, shot from above and cropped to create a full screen of glistening, frosty-blue berries, might be the perfect accompaniment to a series of blueberry dessert recipes or the beginning of a cookbook section on fruit desserts.

### Be Creative

Yes, perfect photos of perfectly prepared dishes can draw people into your cookbook. However, colorful ingredients can be used to create out-of-the-ordinary images that can be both fun and compelling. A woven straw cornucopia with tiny pumpkins, gourds, and nuts spilling out of it might make a nice prelude to a chapter on Thanksgiving dishes. For a chapter on cold soups or salads, you might freeze grape tomatoes, celery stalks, baby carrots, and a few romaine fronds in a block of ice. Grains, legumes, berries, and thick sauces can all be arranged in adjacent wavy stripes on a white background for an interesting photo. If you have a light table, or an opaque glass rack or stand that can be lit from below, try shooting illuminated slices of tomatoes or citrus fruit.

## Making the Best of Found Photos

Not all the pictures in your keepsake cookbook have to be shot by you, and not all the pictures in your book have to be food photos.

First, there are food photographs in the public domain available for your use. Pictures taken or commissioned by government agencies belong to the public.

For example, the Agricultural Research Service of the United States Department of Agriculture has numerous photos on their website, some of which are quite extraordinary. In addition, there are several websites that offer public domain photos, most of which were taken by photographers who uploaded the pictures and gave permission for them to be used by anyone. Food trade associations, such as the National Watermelon Promotion Board, have recipes and photographs available for public use. And finally, many photographers will give permission to use their work—for the price of a credit line—if asked.

**FAST FACTS:** Is it stock or broth? Most cooks use the terms interchangeably. However, technically, stock is made from boiled bones while broth is made by boiling both meat and bones. Another way to look at it is this: Broth is a ready-to-eat product, while stock needs a little doctoring for flavor.

Once you get beyond photographs of ingredients or recipes included in your cookbook, the range of pictures that can supplement your keepsake is extensive. Generic party, scenery, and holiday photos can be found on websites offering public domain photos, as well as on some corporate, city, and state websites. Public libraries and museums often house historic photo collections, and digital copies of the pictures may be available for a nominal fee, usually just enough to cover the cost of handling.

In addition, you have your own photo collection—and the collections of any collaborators—to mine. Consider one or more of the following options:

### Garden-Variety Family Photos

Candid shots of family members at work or at play can be prized additions to any keepsake cookbook, because aside from being interesting to view, they show family activities. A picture of Aunt Rose laughing under the mistletoe would make a fine illustration for her Ambrosia Coffee Cake recipe. Likewise, a picture of an adolescent Dad in a striped uniform, playing shortstop on his Little League baseball team, would be a good conversation starter and a fun picture to drop anywhere in the book.

That said, don't ignore the set-piece photos we all have in our albums: the pictures of all the grandkids in front of the Christmas tree, the snapshot of Grandma and Grandpa on their sixtieth wedding anniversary, the picture of the family lined up at somebody's christening or wedding. Such life-cycle photos document important milestones and give future generations a glimpse of "what everybody looked like" in 1954 or 1983 or whenever. The further back in your family history these pictures reach, the more interesting they become.

## Portraits

Most of us have a box of school pictures lying around someplace, filled with wallet-sized visages of ourselves, our kids and grandkids, cousins, nieces, nephews, and neighbors. Pull a collection of those together to make a collage from a particular era or to show a progression of individual family members.

Antique photos of ancestors often take the form of formal portraits. If you're lucky, you'll find high-contrast black-and-white or sepia-toned pictures of grandparents and great-grandparents in their service uniforms or together in a formal engagement or marriage portrait, or as children in a communion portrait, or suited up to receive some academic, civic, or business honor. Such pictures can be scanned to include in a digital layout or pasted into a hand-built keepsake.

Portraits of a more recent vintage will likely be in color. Use them as is, or scan and save them as black-and-white digital images to arrange side by side with look-alike ancestors.

If your cookbook is based on the culinary exploits of a group or association, a series of portraits of the group's presidents would be a nice nod to the history of the organization.

## A Sense of Place

Look for pictures of the old farmhouse, of Grandpa tilling the field with his mule, of the view from Aunt Josie's Brooklyn brownstone circa 1930, of the gang-of-cousins swinging into the swimming hole from an overhanging oak tree. Places that have significance to your extended family—say, the crowds on St. Charles Avenue on Mardi Gras Day or the Ocean City boardwalk on Memorial Day weekend—make excellent accompaniments to seasonal recipes or just grace notes to make your keepsake much more than a cookbook.

**FAST FACTS:** Saffron is actually the dried stamens of a crocus native to Central Asia and widely used in Mediterranean and Asian cuisines. Since it takes more than 50,000 flowers to make a pound of saffron—and the stamens have to be picked by hand—saffron ranks as the world's most expensive spice. Fortunately, a little goes a long way in dishes like paella and curry.

Place pictures can include friends and family members, or they can be strictly scenery-and-structure images. The rolling fields of a Pennsylvania family farm, the shrimp boat that contributed to the livelihoods of family members, and the bustling, snowy streets of downtown Chicago in winter are all compelling pictures. The important thing is that the image is significant and identifiable to your audience.

## Around the Globe

If your keepsake is going to be part cookbook and part travelogue, your photos should be coordinated with the recipes and stories you plan to tell. Your chapter on France and French food will of course have the photos of the family at the Eiffel Tower, as well as wide-angle shots of the lavender fields of Provence and your artsy compositions from the Lyons train station. In your State Soujourns cookbook, Florida Key lime pie and conch fritter recipes might have photos of the foods being served at an outdoor cafe overlooking the Intracoastal Waterway.

The important thing is to examine your photo collection carefully to come up with the shots that will reproduce best, then make sure you have a good balance of photos representing each type of food and location, and finally, make sure they're photos that capture the essence of your time in each venue.

## Pick a Theme

Group or association keepsake cookbooks will likely reflect the raison d'être of the organization itself. The Springfield Heritage Daylily Society cookbook may have photos of gardens being planted, cuttings being judged, or centerpieces being arranged, but without a doubt it should include beautiful, close-cropped pictures of daylilies in bloom. Similarly, a historic preservation group cookbook might include photos of architecturally significant buildings, and an animal rescue group cookbook will have heart-tugging photos of pets and pets-to-be. Crafters might include pictures of whittled wood toys, handmade quilts, art glass jewelry, or other delights.

But there are other, less obvious themes that can be augmented with photos. Perhaps your cookbook focuses on summer delights and you've decided to create a Fourth of July color theme using pictures with predominant red, white, or blue tones. If you and a group of friends are building a baby shower cookbook, perhaps baby photos of each of you can be part of the mix of pictures. A school keepsake cookbook could take a vintage back-to-school theme and have old school photos set in mats, old school bus pictures, and vintage cafeteria pictures. A holiday menu cookbook can be illustrated with many of the family Christmas, Hanukkah, or New Year's photos you've shot over the years.

## Many Photos, Many Choices

Evaluating your photo collection—both the pictures you have on hand and the ones you can get from collaborators and outside sources—is an important step in creating the keepsake cookbook of your dreams. Think about how often people will enjoy the pictures you select if those photos accompany recipes they use every week. But the photos you use must have an obvious thread, even if it's just "our family through the years," and they must fit with the purpose and theme of the cookbook.

If you're creating a group cookbook, consider naming someone to be the project's photo editor. That person can sort through archives, or through the photos group members submit, to select categories and rankings of pictures. These may include top theme-related, high-quality photos; best theme photos that may be usable in a small size; and decent-quality photos of general interest. From those, you should be able to populate your book or decide to either adjust the theme or dig further for more photos.

While it might be tempting to just throw a bunch of pretty pictures in the book, your efforts will have much greater impact if you select the photos deliberately and leave room for captions or related notes. These features allow you to explain the photos and share your connections to them.

# Collecting Memorabilia: Maps, Ticket Stubs, Invitations, and Documents Help Tell Your Story

Your keepsake cookbook offers a wonderful opportunity for showcasing memories and mementos. An ordinary cookbook might include a few photos and a few cooking tips with recipes. But a keepsake cookbook is all about the connection between food and life. That means the entire spectrum of scrapbook-friendly items—virtually anything that can be presented in two dimensions—can be included.

As with other elements we've discussed, your mementos can be handled in high-tech fashion by first scanning items into your computer and using presentation software or scrapbooking software to create an interesting and attractive layout. Or you can handle these items exactly as you might a handcrafted scrapbook page, making your own cutouts, mats, and layouts. Your pages, paired with typed or handwritten recipes, can be tucked into page protectors for a single book or scanned to make multiple copies.

What makes a good illustration? You might be surprised.

## Children's Artwork

The average elementary school student will bring home hundreds of pieces of hand-drawn art with widely varying themes and levels of clarity. Some of those creative efforts will wind up on your refrigerator. Some will end up in a drawer. And some may even get laminated for placemats. Why not enshrine a few pieces in your cookbook?

Let's say you're putting together a keepsake cookbook featuring all the recipes in your family's Thanksgiving repertoire. Interspersed with recipes and snapshots from extended family get-togethers, you could have a collection of hand-traced turkeys, freehand Pilgrims, and "thankful" drawings from all the children or grandchildren of the family, each with their name and the year the art was produced. For a more general family cookbook, drawings of vegetables, fruit, fish, pizzas, and stick figures eating cookies can all be used to illustrate recipes.

Certainly, a collection of colorful student drawings would be fitting for a group cookbook aimed at children, such as one created for a school fund-raiser or a children's charity. Likewise, a gift cookbook for a teacher might be illustrated with students' artwork. Try including a small photo of the student on the page with the art.

## Maps

Maps make interesting visuals in any book. In a keepsake cookbook, maps can show where you've been or how far your family has come. There are a variety of ways to use maps and a range of map styles that can enhance your particular book. The important thing is to pick the style you wish to use and stick with it.

Primitive, hand-drawn, or traced maps in bright colors can be a charming way to illustrate a family cookbook or one focusing on regional cuisine. For example, a map of Pennsylvania might be segmented into sections, with the area around Kutztown leading a section on sausages; the greater Philadelphia area, antipasto or Italian fare; the Amish country, poultry or vegetables; Pittsburgh, pierogies and Eastern European specialties; and Hershey, desserts.

**FAST FACTS:** It takes about fifteen medium-size whole crabs to equal one pound of crabmeat. That and the labor-intensive process of peeling crabs (they have to be steamed first) explains the high cost of peeled crabmeat.

Similarly, a hand-annotated map can trace the migration pattern of different branches of a family, ending with the current family home. My own family would have lines from three points in Belgium and France, with arrows to Nova Scotia and Louisiana, then additional arrows going from Canada down the Mississippi River to New Orleans and arrows going down the Atlantic coast from Canada to Louisiana.

Cookbooks that showcase recipes collected during travels beg for the addition of a few maps. Classic, clean outline-style maps filled with solid colors would be perfect for a book of recipes collected from specific states, countries, or islands.

Use classic road maps with all the details to serve as mats or borders for your cookbook pages. Make a color copy of a map and paste recipes and mementos onto the page, or scan a map into your computer and insert text boxes with recipes and notes.

One word about legalities: Some maps are copyrighted. Obviously, your own hand-drawn or outline-traced and significantly altered maps belong to you. A map you purchase and cut into segments to use in a single-copy book should also be fine. However, you can't pull any old map from a website and expect it to be freely available. Instead, look for maps from government agencies, which are paid for by taxpayer dollars and available for public use. In addition, some tourist and convention bureau maps may be usable. Check websites for fine print. When in doubt, just send an e-mail and ask for permission to use a map you like. The worst thing that will happen is you'll be turned down or quoted a fee for using the map.

## Family Trees

Your family tree can be an illustration or a unifying theme running through your cookbook. An artsy tree with family branches depicted as actual branches and family members' names inscribed on hanging fruit would be a lovely cover or inside cover illustration for a family cookbook. Or you can adorn different segments of the book with a series of trees, each highlighting different branches of an extended family. This approach works for a small-group cookbook as well as a family cookbook.

If you have a creative bent, you can take poetic license with the concept of a "tree." Consider one of these as an organizational device: a Christmas tree, a Hanukkah menorah, a stylized flowerpot holder bearing pots of herbs, a vertical shelf of cookbooks, a spice rack, or a series of flip-flops in the sand.

For a continuing visual element, you could run a horizontal chart across the bottom of the keepsake cookbook pages. Start with yourself or your immediate family. Then run a line on the next page for the maternal nuclear family and a line on the following page for the paternal nuclear family. Keep extending the lines, alternating ancestor families, throughout the book. Notations might include birth and death years and locations.

The same running chart concept can be used to show the evolution of an organization that has a lengthy history, with events and individuals noted along the track.

**FAST FACTS:** Plant a whole smorgasbord of mint in a container herb garden. Modern cultivars include apple mint, pineapple mint, orange mint, lemon mint, chocolate mint, and, of course, peppermint and spearmint. Keep peppermint and spearmint separate from more delicately flavored mints or they'll take over. And never plant mint in your open garden unless you want a yard full of mint!

## Handwritten Notes and Recipes

It's unlikely that your children will ever consider your grocery-shopping list to be an heirloom. But what if your great-great-great grandfather kept the list of ship stores from the vessel on which he worked his way to the town where he met your great-great-great grandmother? Now that's an heirloom worth keeping. If that list is in a safe full of family documents and treasures, by all means, scan it for posterity and use it to illustrate your keepsake cookbook.

Maybe your grandmother kept all the letters that she and your grandfather exchanged while he was in the service. Those letters, filled with incidental descriptions of time and place as well as loving prose, could be the backdrop for a beautiful keepsake cookbook that would be cherished by all family members. Simply scan the letters and use them, or excerpts from them, throughout the book. Position them alongside photos of your grandparents, their home, and their family. Throw in a few fast facts about the cost of groceries during the time of their courtship and early marriage, about food rationing during the war, and other tidbits specific to the time of the letters.

Any documents of genealogical significance—ship manifests, property deeds, citizenship papers, birth certificates, marriage licenses—can become illustrations for your keepsake. Less-dramatic documents and handwritten items can be used as well. Maybe your family has a tradition of sending one another handmade birthday cards each year. Or perhaps you have a box of handwritten recipes collected from friends and family. Or you might have all the letters your children, nieces, and nephews have written to Santa over the years. All these items can be included in your keepsake, either by attaching hard copy to hand-built pages or by scanning and building into digital pages.

**FAST FACTS:** Family not thrilled by whole grains? Sneak a little health food into meals by using oatmeal in place of bread crumbs in meat loaf, meatballs, and crumb toppings. Oatmeal is high in soluble fiber and helps control cholesterol levels.

## Postcards, Ticket Stubs, and Menus

Do you travel the world every four years to attend the Olympic games? Do you make a pilgrimage to the New Orleans Jazz Festival every year? Or does your dog-rescue group—friends all—make it a point to attend mixed-breed obedience trials together all over the country? Or maybe you just like to travel and enjoy roller coasters, community theater productions, or mom-and-pop restaurants wherever you go.

Memorabilia from your travels can be paired with postcards and your own photos to make interesting page compositions. Souvenirs can range from hotel letterhead to business cards, theater playbills, restaurant menus, event programs, and ticket stubs. Pair the pages with stories from your travels, recipes you collected, or recipes from group members to benefit your cause.

## Original Artwork

If you're a visual artist—a painter, an illustrator, a cartoonist—then by all means use your own creative endeavors to add beauty, charm, and value to your keepsake cookbook. Gift cookbooks in particular would be enhanced by scans of your paintings, especially if your work follows a theme of place or ingredients. For example, your paintings of Chesapeake Bay–area sea creatures and fishing and beach scenes would make a great accompaniment for a mid-Atlantic regional cookbook or a keepsake cookbook that benefits an ecology-devoted nonprofit. Still-life paintings of fruit, peppers, tomatoes, herbs, and other produce collections would be a stunning addition to a personal recipe collection.

A cartoonists' collective might contribute cartoons related to the theme of marriage, children, or pets for a fund-raiser or gift cookbook, while a digital artist could create an animated storyline to connect family cookbook segments.

Two-dimensional craft works—such as quilts, cross-stitch panels, or silk-screened shirts—can be scanned and sized for inclusion in your book. If you're lucky enough to have inherited your grandmother's cross-stitch collection or your grandfather's retirement-era drawings, those would make excellent keepsake cookbook illustrations.

## Event-Specific Memorabilia

If you're putting together a keepsake cookbook for a friend who's getting married, consider this idea: Get all contributors to the cookbook to assemble and scan a page of memorabilia from their own wedding. Include personalized napkins, invitations, wedding or engagement announcements, and photos, creating homage to the institution of marriage. Text boxes can be inserted into the scans to include wishes from the contributor or can serve as a frame for photos.

**FAST FACTS:** Heavy cream is the only liquid dairy product that can be boiled and reduced to a uniform thickness in sauces. Milk and light cream will separate into solids and whey when boiled, which is why soups that contain milk must be simmered but never boiled.

The same approach can be used for a cookbook to celebrate a college graduation, a retirement, or the arrival of a first child.

For a cookbook being produced as a fund-raiser for a small museum, a community theater, a school, or some other nonprofit, a collection of old show or ceremony programs, gala party flyers, and articles related to milestone events can be blended with modern photos and contributors' recipes.

## Handprints, Footprints, Paw Prints

In some cookbooks—for example, a baby shower gift book, a children's cookbook, or a pet rescue benefit cookbook—an accent of a small handprint or baby footprint in a bright color, or a border of small paw prints, might be fun. To get authentic prints (rather than clip art ones), you'll have to press the appendage in question into an ink pad and then press it onto a clean sheet of paper to make the print. From there, the print can be scanned, rendered in different colors, and copied to create whatever effect you like.

## Signatures

A collection of simple signatures, scanned from antique documents or contributed by members of your family or organization, can be used to create powerful page borders or cover panels for your cookbook. Scan the signatures, copy and arrange them on a single document, add an antique linen or other shaded background, and use the sheet as you would a backdrop. Use text boxes to open clear areas for recipes, or just layer mementos over the writing. Use the signatures in different areas, making sure everyone's name appears someplace in the book.

## Botanicals

Press flower petals or herb sprigs between panes of glass to flatten. Then scan or copy these bits of nature to get elements that can be used in your book. Depending on the item and the quality of the copy, you may be able to use the elements in a realistic representation or as an outline that can be filled in with color as desired.

## Scrapbooking Novelties

Whether you're creating your cookbook by hand or digitally, you might consider judicious use of the stickers, icons, and themed photo mats available in scrapbooking departments and scrapbooking software. A lobster sticker might make a nice accent to a page featuring photos from your Ogunquit, Maine, vacation stay, opposite a recipe for saltwater-boiled lobsters. Likewise, an occasional flower, flamingo, college logo, or wagon wheel might be just the thing to pull a page together.

Depending on the theme of your book, paper doilies, fabric squares, or strips of lace might double as mats for your recipes or vintage photos.

Do resist the urge to go wild with such embellishments, because generally speaking, these items aren't meaningful—they're just eye candy.

## Meaningful Visuals

When my Uncle Roy died, his family found boxes and drawers filled with unusual treasures and other items from his life. He had served as a photographer during his tour of duty in World War II, and he was stationed in Italy when Mussolini met his final fate. Although some of the pictures of that day were gruesome, and certainly not cookbook material, there were also documents and snippets of news articles that showed a closer-than-expected connection to the world far outside his hometown.

Combined with scans of maps from some of his domestic travels, details from his rock-hunting hobby, and scans of his very skilled paintings of South Louisiana life, these materials would make an illuminating and interesting backdrop to a section on his favorite dishes and recipes. That assemblage could then be part of a family cookbook or one celebrating World War II veterans of Louisiana. Or it could be part of a cookbook showcasing the heritage of his small town.

Likewise, my cousins—Uncle Roy's children—found *memento mori* items like prayer cards from funerals and a thin frame with a wreath made from our great-grandmother's hair. There also was a wonderful painting my uncle had done of our great-grandmother standing in front of her Cajun cottage in Grand Cotteau, Louisiana. Properly handled, a scan of that painting, with a small scan of the hair wreath and her prayer card and a few biographical details of her life, could lead a section on the recipes our great-grandmother handed down to our grandmother, who gave them to us.

And not to overdo the theme of funerals, but a friend of mine in New Orleans has a collection of jazz funeral memorabilia and photos. Since her family has a history of preparing huge—and I mean groaning—feasts for wakes and after-funeral receptions, my friend wants to merge her collection with her family recipes to make a cookbook to share, preferably not at a funeral.

The point is, many things that you see every day, or things that fall into your life unexpectedly, can give theme, shape, or interest to your keepsake.

# Putting It All Together: High-Tech and Low-Tech Options

Congratulations! You've done all the really hard work on your keepsake cookbook. You've written, gathered, tested, and rewritten recipes. You've interviewed family members or key group members. You've written their stories. You've styled and shot food photos. You've shot special-theme photos. You've collected vintage pictures and memorabilia. In short, you've amassed everything you need to put together the keepsake cookbook you've planned.

Now all you have to do is put it in an attractive, usable package. Remember that it's your cookbook, or your committee's cookbook. It's your gift to those current and future cooks who will benefit from your efforts. So your tastes and preferences should inform the physical presentation of your work. In other words, if you like it, that's really what matters!

That said, this chapter begins with some general content and layout guidelines that you might find helpful. After that, we'll talk about techniques and templates to make your cookbook come to life.

## Be Consistent

Your cookbook is more than a simple collection of recipes. It's a family memoir, a showcase, a history. It's a treasure that people will want to use for cooking, but that they'll also want to curl up and read. That means you'll want to make your layout consistent and predictable so that browsers can gain a level of comfort flipping through the book. Here are some helpful tips.

- Begin all chapters on a right-hand page. The right-hand position in a two-page layout is the stronger position. In most Western cultures, readers are conditioned to think of the right-hand page as a place of "beginning."

- Begin all chapters the same way. You may want to open each chapter with a large photo, a family fable, a quote from a collection of vintage letters, or a historic element. Maybe you have a nice collection of ingredient or finished-dish photos that you'd like to show off at the beginning of the appropriate chapter. Or maybe you have a plan for eight chapters and you've taken eight pictures of your doll collection that could be used to kick off each segment. It really doesn't matter what you choose as long as each chapter begins with the same elements.

- Begin all recipes on the same side of the two-page spreads. Some writers like to begin recipes on the left-hand pages because—particularly with long recipes—the facing right-hand page can be used for additional preparation notes and variations of the dish, keeping the entire package in view without page-turning.

- If you plan to include a note—a memory, food tip, or comment related to your cause or collection—with a recipe, then try to include a similar element with each recipe in the book.

- Essays, profiles, stories, and histories should be placed logically throughout the book, alternating with recipes and illustrations.

## Think "Balance"

- On each two-page spread, arrange elements so they complement one another. Don't overload one area or one page with content while the facing page is nearly empty. An anchor element on the lower outside corner of one page should be balanced with a strong element in the upper outside corner of the facing page.

- Follow the rule of three. Imagine a flexible triangle on each page and place your three primary elements at the corners. Then move the elements in proportion to each other to create a visually pleasing grouping on the page.

- Facing pages should have comparable and comfortable amounts of white space. Don't crowd too many elements onto pages.

## Coordinate Colors

- Pick a color palette for your book and try to stick to it. If your photos or drawings are black-and-white or sepia-toned, your other elements (such as borders and accents) can be more lively shades. If you have color photos, use a limited palette of three colors to keep from overwhelming the photos.

- Remember that your book is meant to be read and used. The recipes should be in dark type on a pale background. Resist the urge to use pastels or different colors of type for your recipes.

- Use the same typeface and color for chapter and section headings. The headings and the recipe fonts can be different from one another, but there should be consistency within the headings and within the recipes.

## High-Tech, Low-Tech, or In Between?

These simple guidelines work for any type of book layout. However, you have to decide, if you haven't already, how you plan to put your cookbook together.

If you have a slush fund devoted to creating and distributing your family or organization cookbook, then by all means, take your concept to a full-service printer in your community and let the staff work their magic. Tell them what you envision, show them some of the elements you've collected, and get an estimate for layout and printing of the number of books you want. Get estimates from several other printers too.

Print-on-demand publishers like Lulu.com can produce single copies of your book in hardcover, soft cover, color, or black and white for prices ranging from a few dollars apiece to more than $30.

**FAST FACTS:** Italian wedding soup can be found at the weddings of North Americans of Italian ancestry. However, in Italy, this popular combination of escarole or spinach, meatballs or sausage, and small pasta in chicken broth is actually known as "married soup," a reference to the marriage of ingredients in the mix.

If your cookbook is destined to be sold as a fund-raiser, you might look into one of the many community cookbook publishers operating in the United States. Some will print cookbooks using your design, while others have their own templates and software.

However, these are all relatively high-cost or high-volume options. To create a personal keepsake cookbook—one that can be distributed to family and friends, or even a circle of enthusiasts—you might want to embrace one of these do-it-yourself options.

## Digital Design, Physical Book

By far, the easiest way to create a keepsake cookbook is the digital design option. Using this method, you load all your cookbook elements into your computer—preferably as you're collecting them—then manipulate the elements onto digital pages. Your recipes, essays, historical references, recipe notes, and profiles can be typed into your system using Microsoft Word or another content-processing software program. Photos can be loaded directly from a digital camera or scanned from hard copy using a home scanner. Artwork, memorabilia, historic documents, and cards can be scanned as well.

Once all the material is loaded into your computer, follow the basic design guidelines regarding color, balance, and consistency and begin creating pages. If you're somewhat tech-savvy, a program like Microsoft Publisher or Adobe InDesign can offer flexibility, a wide range of design options, and the ability to go from the digital page to a professionally printed product with few obstacles.

A less professional but somewhat simpler layout option would be scrapbooking software. For $50 or less, you can buy a scrapbooking program that will allow you to upload your own content into any of several ready-made templates. In addition, these programs offer a large selection of art elements like borders, mats, holiday-themed icons, and fonts to enhance your pages. The trickiest part of using these programs is using restraint. Pull out all the stops and you'll wind up with a hard-to-use collection of busy, uncoordinated pages.

**FAST FACTS:** The dish Polish wedding chicken is actually a Polish-American custom, born of the need to feed large numbers of guests at celebratory meals. Although the dish is simple—chicken pieces, oil, salt, pepper, good paprika, and onions—the result is amazing. The chicken is oven-braised and cooks for almost two hours until everything is golden and meltingly tender.

As we discussed in Chapter 2, the best layout option for most keepsake cookbook authors is presentation software. Programs like PowerPoint, which you probably already have on your computer, can be used to create clean, beautiful pages with clearly defined text, art, and headline areas. The latest editions of these programs feature templates for photo albums and scrapbooks that can be pressed into service for your cookbook.

Browse the templates for something simple and fitting for your particular collection of elements and avoid those that scream "corporate training." Remember that any scanned pieces you've collected can be added to the pages, particularly if you choose an open slide or a slide with a simple border. It's simply a matter of using upload and cut-and-paste features.

Once you've assembled all your keepsake cookbook pages, you can save the presentation as is or save the pages as portable document format (PDF) files for printing. Printing options range from relatively inexpensive to high-end, depending on your desires and your budget. A few possibilities include:

- Printing as many copies as you wish on a home color printer. This option works perfectly well for relatively small books or relatively few copies. Once printed, the pages can be bound into attractive, hardcover books using a home-scale thermal binding unit and covers. Units like the Unibind and Fellowes machines can be purchased at office supply and hobby stores. Less expensive options include manual comb-binding or ring binders.

- Sending the file containing your cookbook pages to a quick-print store and having, for example, FedEx Office or the UPS Store or a local vendor print your book. These vendors have a range of binding options for your book as well.

- Uploading the files to a print-on-demand service for the printing and binding options of your choice.

- Uploading the files to a print-on-demand printer and allowing family, friends, and colleagues to purchase as many copies as they wish.

## Digital Design, Digital Distribution

An alternative option—and a particularly attractive choice for big families where everyone is online—is to save your keepsake cookbook as a PDF book or Power-Point file and e-mail it as an attachment to everyone who would like a copy. If the book file is particularly large, it can be compressed into a .zip file before sending, or sent via a file-sharing service like YouSendIt.com.

Once recipients get a copy of the book, they're free to download it and keep it as an e-book, or print a copy in any manner they choose. This route is economical and eco-friendly. It also works quite well for organizations that would like to sell their cookbook without expending capital. Your digital keepsake cookbook benefiting Happy Trails Equine Rescue can be offered as a prepaid digital download from the organization's website.

To give your digital keepsake as a physical gift, you can download the e-book onto a nicely labeled disk or onto a decorator flash drive.

## Digital Design, Internet Distribution

If your keepsake "book" is to be an ongoing group project, it might make sense to just take it to the web. Do a little research to find a host company that suits your price range and your needs. You should be able to claim a domain name (for example, www.hulinfamilyrecipes.com) for a modest annual fee plus additional fees for hosting services. If your group includes a web-savvy designer, he or she can build the site using contributions from all members. Someone can serve as ongoing webmaster, adding contributions or sections as they develop.

**FAST FACTS:** Who can resist those rich, buttery ball- or crescent-shaped cookies filled with ground pecans or almonds and dusted with confectioners' sugar? Most people know them as Mexican wedding cakes, but they're actually served in many Western cultures and go by many names, including Russian tea cakes, Danish almond cookies, and cocoons. The cookies probably originated with the Moors, who migrated to Spain and shared their love of sugary, almond-laced treats.

If your group is only moderately web-savvy, or is pressed for time, you can look into web authoring tools—available online or in software packages. These tools make site design relatively simple with preset templates, upload features, and a variety of design options.

Your site can be open to anyone surfing the Internet or password protected to allow only approved users.

The important thing to remember is this: Even if all participants have access to an evolving keepsake site, you still need to have defined roles within the group. To make the site attractive and usable, there must be a unifying theme—even if it's just "family and friends share the feast"—and an agreed-upon palette of acceptable elements. The site needs an editor as well as a designer and webmaster to keep things viable and well organized. Finally, there needs to be some agreement as to whether this will be a project/site with an endpoint or continue to evolve over the years.

## Digital Design, "Other"

Your keepsake cookbook doesn't have to be a "book" at all. Once you have some photos or art elements, some notes, and some recipes together, you can create all kinds of vehicles for delivering the information. A photo calendar is a very nice way to put together a limited number of recipes of a single genre—think soups, or cookies, or pies. You'll have room for a food or family photo, a recipe, and a little remembrance or quote, in addition to the actual calendar page. This works for family calendars (you may even be able to include birthdays and family anniversaries on the date grid) or organization calendars. Imagine a calendar called "Beauty and the Feast" for a rose enthusiasts' club. Beautiful rose photos and growing tips, recipes from the organization's potluck dinners, and facts about the history of the organization could make this a lovely favor for members, or even a fund-raising item.

Another option would be a series of greeting cards or a collection of small prints or posters.

Use existing software on your computer, software you purchase, or an online photo product site to make your vision a reality.

## Old-School Manual Design, Physical Book

Maybe you're not comfortable with digital design, or maybe you just want the tactile experience of putting your keepsake together by hand. If you have patience and a lot of original photographs, documents, and other elements that you want to showcase in a one-of-a-kind keepsake, it might make sense to create a handmade scrapbook-cookbook.

Unless you plan to render your recipes in calligraphy or you have a perfectly consistent printing style, you'll want to type your recipes—following the guidelines in Chapter 4—to make them clear and easy-to-read. Set the margins on your word processing software or typewriter to keep all the recipes similarly situated on individual pages. You can then cut out, mat, or border the pages using your preferred design elements. In a perfect world, your recipes will be consistently situated in one area of either right- or left-hand pages in your book.

Use a base of acid-free, archival paper for your book and opt for a size that will easily accommodate the original documents and photos you wish to use. Design pages according to general design guidelines, balancing elements, allowing for fluid eye movements, and using scrapbooking-style embellishments judiciously. Use fasteners that will not damage original documents and art elements like birth certificates, vintage photos, and original drawings.

Load your keepsake cookbook pages into page protectors to keep kitchen spills and fingerprints from damaging your work. Layer protectors in a scrapbook or decorated binder.

Once the book is completed, I strongly suggest going to a self-service print shop and making color copies of each page. Even if the book is for your own use and enjoyment, a copy will give you a document that you won't mind using in the kitchen or passing around to friends and family. If you'd like to share your work, you can make several photocopies of the pages and load them into attractive binders. Or you can have your original work scanned into a digital file that friends and family members can download from a disk, flash drive, or e-mail attachment.

**FAST FACTS:** In New Orleans, before the wedding cake is cut, unmarried girlfriends of the bride gather for the traditional ribbon pulling. White ribbons extend from a tier of the cake, with one end buried in the icing. The hidden end is attached to a charm—usually a ring, a dime, a thimble, a button, a heart, and a few other possibilities. At once (usually right after a group photo) each of the girls pulls her ribbon. The charms represent future prospects!

## Managing Costs

The chief initial expenditure in creating a keepsake cookbook is time. It's a labor of love, mostly dependent on your willingness to collect, edit, and assemble the components. However, as anyone who ever walked the aisles of a craft store or browsed the web for hobby software knows, it's easy to get carried away with all the accoutrements of a newfound passion. The way to avoid buying toys and tools you don't need is to create your blueprint, adjust it as needed along the way, and invest only in what you need to realize your keepsake cookbook dream.

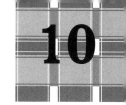

# Keep a Good Thing Going:
# Your Evolving Table

You're almost there! At this point in the keepsake cookbook process, one of two things has happened. Either you are on the verge of packaging the keepsake of your dreams, or you've gotten stymied somewhere along the way.

If you're among the stymied, don't worry. Chances are you had a big, beautiful vision, stumbled a little, and ran out of time or energy. As your official cheering squad, I'm here to tell you not to give up. And to tell you that you don't have to create this imposing project all at once.

Look at what you have, or what you can easily get your hands on right now. Maybe you found a cache of your grandfather's pickle recipes. Not only that, you have a photo of him making pickles, as well as a few pictures of family around the dinner table at his house. You remember the stories your mother and her sisters told about Granddad's hot chow-chow, his pickled okra, his garlicky dills, and how he invited his grandchildren to watch his "secret" process.

Those elements alone would make a wonderful small keepsake, devoted to one person, one topic. You can put it together, get it bound into a lovely little book, and distribute it to grateful cousins, aunts, and uncles.

Or maybe the things you've collected don't seem quite so rare. Maybe you just have the meat loaf your husband loves, the über-rich baked macaroni and cheese recipe you got from your sister-in-law, the red beans and rice you learned to make after a trip to New Orleans, and a few other down-home family favorites. Heirloom recipes? Maybe not to you. But to your children and their cousins and friends, they will be. In a blink, the "kids" will be heading off to college or to their first apartment and they'll be asking for those recipes. Wouldn't it be great to start putting those simple soul-nourishing recipes together, along with your favorite life lessons and practical tips that you learned while juggling tasks and making meals? Start with a little e-book called *Family Favorites*. Include all the comfort food that makes people migrate to your table. As time goes on, add sections: the birthday cakes your children love, your neighbor's special cranberry coleslaw, the slow-cooked brisket recipe you finally perfected. At some point you'll have that fabulous keepsake cookbook of your dreams. But long before that, you'll have a collection of recipes that can be shared.

Or maybe your plans for a church fund-raiser cookbook fizzled when one of the three key players on the committee got transferred out of town. No problem. Put together a dozen or so recipes, along with anecdotes about the contributors and some inspirational sayings related to food and nourishment, put them into a digital file, and get permission to load the file onto the church website. Along with the link to the file, include a downloadable form for anyone interested in contributing to the church's cookbook. Ask them to include a recipe, an explanation about why the recipe is a favorite, a memory about the church or its leaders, or a moment when they were inspired. Give instructions for them to e-mail the form as an attachment to an e-mail account you set up for that purpose. In a few months, you'll have all the recipes and stories you need to create a cookbook that everyone in the congregation—and all their friends—will want to buy.

For example:

Name: _____

Address: _____

Phone number: _____

E-mail: _____

Congregation: _____


Favorite recipe: _____

Category: _____

Title: _____

Ingredients: _____

Instructions:_____

Serves:_____

Ethnic origin of the dish: _____


Why you love this recipe:` _____

Your favorite memory involving St. Paul's: _____

Your favorite "people" memory of church leaders or congregation members: _____

How the church has nourished you: _____

## Stress Is Bad for Digestion

Don't be despondent over the gap between your vision and what you have achieved so far. The important thing is to use what you've collected and keep some momentum going. That Christmas cookie cookbook can become the first in a series of small dessert cookbooks, or the first in a series of holiday cookbooks. Eventually it can become one chapter in a large family keepsake cookbook.

Now, for those of you who have almost realized your vision—and who now have a collection of hundreds of recipes, stories, and photographs—let me suggest a way to spread the wealth without breaking the bank. Put your book together in digital or manual form, but arrange the chapters in logical segments that can stand alone if needed. For example, your family cookbook could have traditional chapters, or segments such as party foods, family favorites, Thanksgiving feasts, preserves and pickles, and perfect pies. Or maybe you can divide your keepsake cookbook into eras: the County Kilkenny years, the Brooklyn years, the Philadelphia years, the Ocala years. Then you have the option of issuing your cookbook to friends and family in a series, which will give them something to look forward to over a period of months or even years.

If you have all the materials collected for a group cookbook but aren't sure you want to make the commitment to have it printed, consider producing an e-book. You can put the book together digitally, save it as a PDF file, and offer it as a simple download from your group website using PayPal or some other electronic payment service. Or you can use a commercial e-book publisher like Smashwords, Untreed Reads, or even Amazon.com. As long as you maintain the copyright, there's no reason you can't decide to publish the book in hard copy later.

## Embrace Instant Gratification

If it seems like I'm focusing on getting something—even if it's incomplete—out of your kitchen and off your desk as soon as possible, you're absolutely right. Cookbooks are meant to be used and enjoyed. That said, the reason I want you to issue *something* is because that something will lead to a better cookbook in the future.

From my own experience, I can tell you that some people need to see a physical entity before they get on board. When I wrote *Roux Memories,* I let many, many people know what I was doing. When I asked for information, some relatives and friends were very forthcoming; others claimed to have nothing I could use. Once the book came out, those who professed to have "nothing" suddenly found photos, recipes, and stories that would have been wonderful additions to the book. They weren't holding out—they simply didn't understand what I was trying to do. Now when I expand on the family cookbook, I'll have even more material to work with.

As soon as you produce a cookbook, you'll find many more contributors than you had originally and the original contributors will come forth with even more material. This is why I like to encourage writers to think of their keepsake cookbook as a living document, something that will expand in breadth and depth. Maybe you will produce the original document and go on to create future editions, or maybe your brother, daughter, or another member of your group will pick up the mantle. The important thing is that your culinary heritage is being curated.

## Preserving the Past, Saving the Future

Ultimately, keepsake cookbooks are fun, functional tools. Some people will take your cookbook and follow the recipes exactly. Others will read the book and get a craving for some dish from their childhood. They'll head to the kitchen, use your recipe as a guide, and work until the dish tastes the way they remember it. The important thing is that a keepsake cookbook encourages people to go back to the kitchen to reclaim their cuisine.

That is my goal in this effort. Not only do I want people to keep their recipes and their histories alive, but I also want them to bring life back to their tables. My theory, born of anecdotal evidence and my own experience, is that homemade food and food that has a connection to one's past is more likely to be shared with others at a common sitting. I firmly believe that's a good thing.

Browsing a US government website recently, I came to a page talking about the importance of families eating dinner together. Research results showed that girls who eat dinner with family five times a week were much less likely to develop eating disorders, and all children who have regular family meals were less likely to develop substance abuse problems.

All of that made sense, but the section of the web page that stopped me cold was a series of bullet points addressing the question of what to talk about at the family dinner table. In other words, the assumption was that we eat dinner as families so seldom that we no longer know how to have basic conversation with one another.

Barely a generation ago, most people learned how to behave at the table by participating in family meals. They learned the art of conversation, family lore, and manners. They also learned to have certain expectations about what a meal offers in terms of substance and sustenance. Eating with others is comforting, but it's also socializing. It tells us who we are—by the dishes on the table—and it teaches us how to interact with others.

I'm not immune to the pressures of the modern household. I can assure you that the pizza delivery guy knows how to find my house, and I've brought home my share of food gathered from a drive-through window. My family juggles work, school, activities, and social obligations just like most families. But I also believe that if we don't come back to the table—instead of eating over the sink, in the car, or by the light of the refrigerator—that we're going to lose something very important.

## The Keepsake Difference

Ironically, today there are many, many venues and forums online for collecting recipes. There are still hundreds of cookbooks on bookstore and library shelves. Yet those recipes alone don't seem to be encouraging family dinners, dinner parties, or coffee klatches. Cooks may find new recipes to be fun or a challenge, but the occasional new recipe or idea isn't likely to change behavior.

The keepsake cookbook—with its photos, mementos, and memories—offers more than just a recipe or a menu idea. It gives us food with a connection to our lives. That's a powerful thing, maybe powerful enough to make us want to share.

# Appendix I: Printing and Digital Resources

## Cookbook Printing and Production Companies

**Morris Press Cookbooks**
3212 E. Highway 30
Kearney, NE 68847
www.morriscookbooks.com

**Wimmer Cookbooks**
4650 Shelby Air Drive
Memphis, TN 38118
www.wimmerco.com

**Fundcraft Publishing**
410 Highway 72 West
Collierville, TN 38017
www.fundcraft.com

**The Cookbook Company**
1146 N. Central Avenue, #458
Glendale, CA 91202
www.cookbookco.com

## Online Publishing Resources

**The Great Family Cookbook Project**
www.familycookbookproject.com

**CreateSpace Self-Publishing**
www.createspace.com

**Lulu**
www.lulu.com

**Blurb**
www.blurb.com

**Smashwords**
www.smashwords.com

**Untreed Reads**
www.untreedreads.com

**iUniverse**
www.iuniverse.com

**Xlibris**
www.xlibris.com

## Cookbook and Scrapbook Software Packages

**Nova Development**
www.novadevelopment.com

**The Cookbook People**
www.cookbookpeople.com

**ValuSoft**
www.valuesoft.com

**Hallmark**
www.hallmarksoftware.com

# Appendix II: Gifts from the Kitchen

Your keepsake cookbook—whether produced exclusively by you or by a group that includes you—will be a treasure for your family and friends. Believe me when I tell you that you'll wind up giving several as gifts. And, when a cookbook becomes a gift, there's nothing better than getting it accompanied by a small sampling from the recipes. Include any of the recipes below in your cookbook. Then, when the time comes to give your keepsake as a gift, make a little gift bag or basket that includes these very-giftable items. Or include giftable dishes of your own devising.

## Old-Fashioned Fifteen-Bean Soup Mix

1 cup dried black beans
1 cup dried small red beans
1 cup dried kidney beans
1 cup dried great northern beans
1 cup dried navy beans
1 cup dried pinto beans
1 cup dried calico beans
1 cup dried baby lima beans
1 cup dried lima beans
1 cup dried black-eyed peas
1 cup dried garbanzo beans
1 cup dried green split peas
1 cup dried yellow split peas
1 cup dried brown lentils
1 cup dried field peas
½ cup granulated chicken bouillon

*1 tablespoons dried Italian herbs*
*2 tablespoons chili powder*
*2 tablespoons dehydrated onion flakes*
*½ tablespoon dehydrated celery*
*2 tablespoons kosher salt*
*1 tablespoon red pepper flakes*
*1 tablespoon garlic powder*
*2 teaspoons black pepper*
*2 teaspoons cumin*

1. Examine each cup of beans and discard any bits of stone or discolored beans. Mix all the beans together in a very large bowl or pot. Divide well-mixed beans into eight pint jars. Cover tightly.

2. In a small bowl, combine chicken bouillon and seasonings together. Divide seasonings into eight small resealable plastic bags.

3. Print soup preparation instructions on a small card. Attach bags to the cards and package the bags and cards with the soup jars using decorative cloth covers or ribbons. Or print the instructions on decorative stick-on labels and press on the jars.

**Soup instructions:**

Pour 1 pint jar of beans into a strainer. Rinse well. Place in a soup pot with 1 packet seasonings and 8 cups of water. Add ½ pound smoked sausage, diced ham, or smoked turkey and bring to a boil. Reduce heat to low and simmer 3 hours, stirring often. Adjust seasonings and serve.

MAKES 8 PINTS OF BEAN SOUP MIX. EACH PINT SERVES 4.

*Note:* For a spicier soup, add a can of tomatoes and green chilies to the pot.

## Spiced Crackers

1¼ cups vegetable oil

½ teaspoon onion powder

1 teaspoon garlic powder

2 tablespoons red pepper flakes

1 1-ounce package powdered ranch or garlic-and-herb salad dressing mix

1 16-ounce box saltine crackers, unsalted tops

1. In a bowl or large measuring cup, whisk together oil, onion powder, garlic powder, red pepper flakes, and salad dressing packet. Let stand 1 hour, then whisk again to blend well.

2. Place crackers, slightly overlapping, in a large roaster or Dutch oven. Drizzle the oil mixture over the crackers. Using your hands, gently mix the crackers with the oil, making sure all the crackers are coated. Let stand in the pan until the crackers have absorbed the marinade and are dry.

3. Package the crackers in tightly closed tins.

MAKES 4 SMALL GIFT TINS OF CRACKERS.


## Lemon Squares

2⅓ cups flour, divided use

⅔ cup confectioners' sugar, divided use

¼ teaspoon salt

1 cup chilled butter

6 eggs

2½ cups sugar

½ cup fresh lemon juice

1 tablespoon grated lemon zest

½ teaspoon baking powder

1. Preheat oven to 350°F.

2. Combine 2 cups flour, ½ cup confectioners' sugar, and salt. Add cold butter. Cut mixture together with a pastry blender or two knives until coarse crumbs form. Press mixture into a buttered 9 x 12-inch pan. Pierce holes in the pastry with a fork. Bake at 350°F for 15 minutes or until crust just begins to brown. Remove from oven.

3. Whisk together remaining flour plus eggs, sugar, lemon juice, lemon zest, and baking powder until thick and well blended. Pour mixture over crust and spread evenly.

4. Bake at 350°F for 20 to 25 minutes or until lemon filling sets. Remove from oven and allow to cool completely.

5. Sprinkle remaining confectioners' sugar over the lemon layer. Cut into squares.

MAKES 16 SQUARES.

## Mini Pumpkin Pound Cakes

*1 pound unsalted butter, softened*

*3 cups sugar*

*6 eggs*

*1 cup buttermilk*

*1 teaspoon vanilla extract*

*2 teaspoons cinnamon*

*¼ teaspoon cloves*

*¼ teaspoon powdered ginger or nutmeg*

*2 teaspoons baking powder*

*3½ cups flour*

*½ teaspoon salt*

*1 cup pumpkin puree*

*1 cup confectioners' sugar*

*3 tablespoons heavy cream*

*¼ teaspoon almond or vanilla extract*

*1 cup chopped pecans*

1. In a large mixing bowl, blend butter and sugar with an electric mixer at medium speed until creamy. Add eggs one at a time, mixing well after each addition.

2. Combine buttermilk and vanilla. In a separate bowl, whisk together cinnamon, cloves, ginger or nutmeg, baking powder, flour, and salt.

3. Add half the flour mixture to the butter and eggs and beat at medium speed until well blended. Slowly add the buttermilk and vanilla, and mix well. Add the remaining flour mixture and beat well. Batter should be thick and smooth.

4. Beat in the pumpkin puree until evenly distributed throughout the batter.

5. Divide pound cake batter among six buttered mini Bundt pans or six buttered miniature loaf pans. Bake at 350°F for 20 to 25 minutes or until a tester comes out clean. Allow cakes to cool in the pan for 15 minutes, then turn onto cooking racks. Cool completely.

6. Whisk together confectioners' sugar, heavy cream, and extract until smooth. Drizzle over the cakes and sprinkle with nuts.

MAKES 6 SMALL GIFT CAKES.


## Raspberry Cheesecake Brownie Bites

**Brownie base:**

*1 package dark chocolate or chocolate chunk brownie mix*

*1 egg*

*¼ cup oil*

*¼ cup water*

## Topping:

*8 ounces cream cheese, softened*

*¼ cup confectioners' sugar*

*1 egg*

*½ cup raspberry jam*

1.  Preheat oven to 350°F.

2.  In a large bowl, combine brownie mix, egg, oil, and water. Whisk until well blended and all brownie mix is moistened. Spoon brownie mixture into 24 paper-lined mini muffin cups.

3.  With a mixer, beat cream cheese, confectioners' sugar, and egg until creamy. Carefully spoon cream cheese mixture over the brownie batter. Drop a small amount of raspberry jam (scant ½ teaspoon) into the center of the cream cheese batter on each brownie bite.

4.  Bake at 350°F until the cream cheese is lightly browned, about 10 to 15 minutes. Cool in the tins, then remove to a platter to cool completely before packaging.

MAKES 24 MINI MUFFINS.


## Bourbon Pecan Squares

**Crust:**

*2 cups flour*

*½ cup sugar*

*2 tablespoons ground pecans*

*1 cup chilled butter*

*⅛ teaspoon salt*

**Filling:**

*4 eggs*

*⅓ cup melted butter*

*⅓ cup corn syrup*

*½ cup sugar*

*⅓ cup brown sugar*

*2–3 tablespoons bourbon*

*Pinch salt*

*2 cups chopped, toasted pecans*

**Make crust:**
1. In a large bowl, combine flour, sugar, ground pecans, butter, and salt. With a pastry blender or two knives, work the butter into the dry ingredients until the mixture resembles coarse meal.

2. Turn dough into a well-greased 9 x 13-inch glass baking pan. With floured fingers, press dough evenly across the bottom of the pan. Prick top of crust with a fork and bake at 350°F for 15 to 20 minutes. Allow to cool slightly.

**Make filling:**
1. With a mixer on low speed or a whisk, whip together eggs, melted butter, corn syrup, sugar, brown sugar, bourbon, and salt. Stir in pecans.

2. Pour mixture over the top of the crust and bake at 350°F for 20 to 25 minutes or until top is browned and set. Remove from oven to cool. Cut into 24 squares or diamond shapes.

MAKES 24 SQUARES OR DIAMONDS.

## Cashew Brittle

*½ cup light corn syrup*
*½ cup water*
*1 cup sugar*
*2½ cups roasted cashews*
*1 teaspoon baking soda*

1. In a heavy pot, combine corn syrup, water, and sugar. Place over medium heat and stir to combine. Add cashews. Cook, stirring constantly, until nuts begin to make a popping sound, about 5 minutes. Add baking soda and cook, stirring, for 3 more minutes.

2. Pour hot brittle into a large buttered baking pan. Cool completely, then break into pieces. Store in an airtight container.

MAKES 16 LARGE PIECES.

## Cointreau Truffles

½ cup whipping cream
2 tablespoons Cointreau
12 ounces good-quality bittersweet chocolate, broken in small pieces
⅔ cup cocoa powder
⅔ cup finely chopped pecans or almonds

1. In a saucepan, heat whipping cream to scalding, stirring occasionally. Stir in Cointreau.

2. Place chocolate in a heat-safe bowl and pour hot cream mixture over the broken chocolate. Stir until the chocolate is melted and the mixture is smooth. Cover and refrigerate until well chilled.

3. Line a baking pan with waxed paper. Working quickly, scoop out a teaspoonful of the chocolate mixture and roll into a ball with your hands. Drop the ball onto the waxed paper. Repeat until all the chocolate mixture is used up. Refrigerate for at least 2 hours.

4. Pour the cocoa powder on one plate and the nuts on another. Roll half the balls in cocoa and half in nuts. Return to the lined pan and refrigerate until ready to serve or package. Keep packaged truffles as cool as possible.

MAKES 30 TRUFFLES.

## Holiday Spice Mix

1 cup sugar
1 vanilla bean, split
¾ cup ground cinnamon
1 tablespoon powdered ginger
1 tablespoon ground nutmeg
½ tablespoon ground cloves
½ tablespoon ground cardamom
½ tablespoon allspice
½ tablespoon ground anise

1. Pour sugar into a large jar with a tight-fitting lid. Press vanilla bean halves into the sugar and cover the container. Let stand 3 to 6 days.

2. Remove vanilla beans and reserve for another use. Add remaining spices to the jar, cover, and shake vigorously to blend.

3. Using a small funnel, divide the spice blend into eight 2-ounce jars or very small resealable plastic bags. Can be used to spice warm drinks, top cookies and muffins, or coat sweets.

MAKES 2 CUPS SPICE OR 8 GIFT PACKAGES.

*Note:* Anise gives the mix a mild licorice flavor. If you prefer to omit the anise, just substitute more cinnamon or sugar.

## Pepper-Lime Vodka

1 750-ml bottle vodka
2 jalapeño peppers, seeded and quartered
1 scotch bonnet pepper, seeded and quartered
1 lime, sliced

1. Pour vodka into a large, clean jar with a tight-fitting lid. Add peppers and lime. Cover tightly.

2. Let stand 3 days at room temperature, swirling ingredients occasionally.

3. Strain vodka into another jar, then use a funnel to pour the vodka into a decorative bottle or flasks.

MAKES APPROXIMATELY 3 HALF-PINTS.

*Pesto Trio*
## Classic Pesto Sauce

*2 cups fresh basil leaves*
*4 garlic cloves, chopped*
*½ cup pine nuts*
*⅔ cup grated Parmesan cheese (or mix of Parmesan and Romano)*
*½ cup extra-virgin olive oil*
*Cracked black pepper to taste*

1. Combine basil, garlic, pine nuts, and cheese in the work bowl of a food processor fitted with a metal blade. Pulse until ingredients are uniformly chopped.

2. With the food processor running, pour the olive oil into the work bowl in a thin, steady stream. Process just until mixture is well blended. Add black pepper as desired. Toss with hot pasta, or add to cream sauces, tomato sauces, or soups.

MAKES 1 GENEROUS CUP PESTO SAUCE.

## Cilantro-Pecan Pesto

*2 cups fresh cilantro leaves*
*2 garlic cloves, chopped*
*1 green onion, chopped*
*½ cup toasted pecans*
*½ cup grated, aged manchego cheese*
*1 small red hot pepper, optional*
*½ cup extra-virgin olive oil*

1. Combine cilantro, garlic, green onion, pecans, and cheese in the work bowl of a food processor fitted with a metal blade. Add pepper if using. Pulse until ingredients are uniformly chopped.

2. With the food processor running, pour the olive oil into the work bowl in a thin, steady stream. Process just until mixture is well blended. Add to sauces, soups, or chicken dishes or to flavor cheese quesadillas.

MAKES ABOUT 1 CUP PESTO SAUCE.

**Sun-Dried Tomato-Parsley Pesto**

*1 cup fresh, flat-leaf parsley leaves*
*1 cup drained oil-packed sun-dried tomatoes*
*3 garlic cloves, chopped*
*½ cup toasted pine nuts*
*½ cup grated Asiago cheese*
*½ teaspoon red pepper flakes*
*½ cup extra-virgin olive oil*

1. Combine parsley, sun-dried tomatoes, garlic, and pine nuts in the work bowl of a food processor. Pulse until ingredients are coarsely chopped. Add cheese and red pepper flakes. Pulse to blend.

2. With the food processor running, pour olive oil into the work bowl in a thin, steady stream. Process just until mixture is well blended. Add to soups, toss with hot pasta, or serve as a topping for bruschetta.

MAKES 1 GENEROUS CUP PESTO.

**Prepare gift:**

Divide each batch of pesto into two half-cup jars that seal tightly. Refrigerate until ready to use. Include one jar in a gift basket, or package three varieties of pesto together to make a gift pack. Give with fresh baguettes or handmade dried pasta as a hostess gift. Include instructions to refrigerate the pesto promptly.

MAKES 2 HALF-CUP JARS OF EACH VARIETY.

# Index

# Index

Pepper-Lime Vodka, 162
Poached Salmon, 81–82
Pot Roast, 74–75
Rasberry Cheesecake Brownie
    Bites, 158–59
Roasted Chicken, 77
Rosemary-Garlic Tenderloin of
    Beef, 77–78
Sautéed Broccoli, 83–84
Senate White Bean Soup, 71–72
Shrimp Creole, 80–81
Simple Chili with Beans, 73–74
Spiced Crackers, 156
Steamed Long Grain White or
    Jasmine Rice, 83
Sugar Cookies, 91
Sun-Dried Tomato-Parsley
    Pesto, 164
Whole Cranberry Sauce, 71
*Recipes from Southern Kitchens,* 8
*Roux Memories: A Cajun-Creole Love
    Story with Recipes* (Hulin), 15, 28,
    44, 53–54, 109, 112–16, 149–50

*Seasonal Florida,* 9
Serif, Ltd., 24
Smashwords, 149
StoryRock, 24

tidbits and fast facts
    adding alcohol to dishes, 81
    ambrosia, 111
    baking powder, 19
    bestselling cookbooks, 7
    bride's cakes and groom's cakes, 89
    cast iron pots, 30
    catfish, 124
    chili powder, 33
    Chinese wedding celebrations, 42
    cookbook collections by American
        women, 6

cookies, 144
corkscrews, 75
cornbread, 118
crabmeat, 132
cranberries, 29
earliest surviving collection of
    recipes, 2
evaporated milk, 24
first American-made china used
    in the White House, 121
first book written by an African
    American author, 5
Floridians and the first
    Thanksgiving meal, 59
heavy cream, 136
herbs, 25
Historic American Cookbook
    Project collection, 5
Italian wedding soup, 141
Junior League cookbooks, 8
Memphis in May festival and
    the World Championship
    Barbecue Cooking Contest, 53
mint, 133
New Orleans and the St. Patrick's
    Day parade, 45
New Orleans and wedding cakes,
    145
oatmeal, 135
olive oils, 37
oven temperatures and cracked
    cake layers, 119
Pennsylvania Dutch cooks, 47
pineapple juice and chicken, 38
Pliny the Elder, 10
Polish wedding chicken, 142
quick mocha brownies, 34
religious orders and the making of
    spirits, 90
Russian River Brewery and India
    Pale Ale (IPA), 10

saffron, 128
starting a microbrewery, 108
State Dining Room in the White
    House, 121
stocks and broths, 127
substitute for buttermilk, 15
tequila, 105
tomatoes, 16
truffle-hunting grounds, 62
vegetable soup, 23
whiskey, 101
wild boars, 125

Untreed Reads, 149
US Copyright Office, 53

Warshaw, Robin, 2
*White Iris* (O'Dell), 7
writing recipes
    abbreviations, 47–48
    clarifying best ingredients for
        recipe, 50
    copyrights, 53
    deciphering heirloom and ethnic
        recipes and terms you may
        encounter, 57–62
    dividing into categories, 43–44
    format for recipes, 54–55
    giving proper credit, 53–56
    including recipe yields, 52–53
    listing ingredients in the order of
        use, 45–47
    measurements, 48–50
    testing recipes, 56
    writing instructions clearly and
        logically, 51–52
    writing usable recipes, 44–53

# About the Author

Belinda Hulin is a five-time cookbook author as well as a veteran food writer. In *Roux Memories: A Cajun-Creole Love Story with Recipes* (Lyons Press, 2010), Hulin chronicles her South Louisiana family through food, vintage photos, and essays. The devastation of Hurricane Katrina, and the near loss of treasured recipes, prompted her to document the family taste-print for future generations. Now, she passionately urges others to write their own memoir cookbooks. She wrote *The Keepsake Cookbook: Gathering Delicious Memories One Recipe at a Time* as a step-by-step guide. Hulin lives in Atlantic Beach, Florida, with her husband, Jim Crissman, and their children, Dylan and Sophie.